# GRRR!

# GRRR!

## The Complete Guide to Understanding and Preventing Aggressive Behavior in Dogs

### Mordecai Siegal and Matthew Margolis

**Little, Brown and Company**
Boston   New York   London

First Edition

Pen-and-ink sketches by Cynthia Holmes, with additional sketches by Steve Miglio.

Library of Congress Cataloging-in-Publication Data

Siegal, Mordecai.
     Grrr! : the complete guide to understanding and preventing aggressive behavior in dogs / by Mordecai Siegal and Matthew Margolis. — 1st ed.
         p.   cm.
     ISBN 0-316-79022-2
     1. Dogs — Behavior.   2. Dogs — Training.   3. Aggressive behavior in animals.   I. Margolis, Matthew.   II. Title.
     SF433.S56   2000
     636.7'0887 — dc21                                          99–14310

10   9   8   7   6   5   4   3   2   1

Book design: Barbara Werden Design

MV-NY

Printed in the United States of America

# Contents

# Introduction

"GRRR!" That is the sound of an aggressive dog that may be a sweet and loving friend until he feels challenged or threatened. The "best friend" concept goes out the window when your dog's behavior makes you want to change his name from Honeybun to Satan. Your best friend should be a happy, gentle companion, sharing your life and bringing more love into it. Your dog should not be barking excessively, growling, nipping, or, God forbid, biting. Many dogs are too aggressive and may even be dangerous for humans or other dogs who come in contact with them. Aggressive behavior is disruptive, upsetting, and sometimes dangerous. It is not what living with a dog is supposed to be like.

Beware of the puppy that growls when you try to touch his food bowl or nips your fingers in a sudden, snapping manner. What appears to be cute and harmless in a young dog has the potential for growing into a serious problem as the dog grows older and larger. Aggressive behavior in dogs takes many forms. Some dogs bully well-intentioned people with intimidating body language and menacing barks and growls. Some dogs run after innocent people and chase them away, while others block their paths. Threatening behavior from a dog is serious. Pet owners must deal with it quickly and decisively.

In most cases, the situation is correctable. Dog owners and those who wish to become dog owners need competent advice and instruction. With this in mind, we have attempted to fill this important and urgent need.

People who do not live with dogs cannot understand why some dog owners expect them to accept the aggressive behavior of their pets. There is a strong, growing reaction against aggressive dogs and owners who refuse to confront the issue of aggressive behavior. This reaction has brought about a great deal of anti-dog legislation that attempts to place severe limits on breeding and owning, and even attempts to ban specific breeds. We hope to make a contribution to responsible dog ownership in order to help change the negative feelings developing toward all dogs and their families.

The important contributions made to society, as well as to individuals, by dogs and those who breed, doctor, train, and employ them are self-evident. Ask blind, deaf, or other disabled persons who have dogs to assist them. Ask those languishing in nursing homes, invalids, disabled patients, mental patients, prison inmates, hospitalized children, and all the others who feel hopeful and loved when therapy dogs come to call on them. Ask police departments, bomb squads, search and rescue teams, and military units whose dogs save their lives in combat. Ask pet owners about their dogs, and they will tell you how their lives are nourished every day by the love, friendship, and companionship they receive so freely from the best "members of their family."

The problem is that some dogs are born aggressive and others are made aggressive. It is important to understand that even the sweetest dog can become aggressive in certain circumstances, if the conditions are right. In many cases a dog that is wonderful in every way may have a consistently bad response to one specific situation or person. If you change the situation and correct the bad response, the dog may become *totally* wonderful. Apart from the fact that aggressive behavior in dogs is nasty and unpleasant, it also has the potential to be dangerous for everyone, especially children. So-called junkyard dogs or even the larger purebred dogs encouraged to be aggressive are not the only dogs that can be dangerous. The smallest dog can be threatening if not handled properly. Big dogs. Little dogs. They all have teeth, and they all can bite.

Once a dog has bitten someone, he has crossed a behavioral threshold that should make it clear to the owners that they must do something before things get worse. Some dog owners deny that anything is wrong and refuse to see their situation realistically until it is too late. For some the situation seems hopeless because of the false impression that the only options available are to get rid of their dogs or to live with the consequences, requiring them to pay large sums of money for injuries to others. It is an emotionally charged dilemma, especially for those who love their dogs, aggressive or not.

Unfortunately, the desperate pet owner's first response to aggressive behavior is to isolate their dog and lock him away from everyone and everything, in the garage or the basement or in a confining dog run. It is a form of solitary confinement. The owner soon discovers that this only worsens the dog's behavior and completely eliminates the joy of living with a pet. But there is help available. In many situations it is the owner who can change aggressive behavior, or it can be changed by a professional dog trainer.

No matter what the outcome may be, it is essential for those who own such dogs to understand all their options and how to exercise them. How else can they do the right thing? In the following chapters troubled dog owners are offered useful and enlightening information about aggressive canine behavior, the various forms it takes, and the necessity for doing something about it. Of great importance are the techniques for preventing, managing, and modifying (where possible) this upsetting and potentially dangerous behavior of a much loved member of the family. But of even greater importance is the willingness to acknowledge a dog's aggressive behavior and identify it in the most specific sense possible.

The purpose of this book is to familiarize the dog owner with the variations of aggressive canine behavior and offer some help with coping with it. This information could make a difference to the family that loves its dog despite his upsetting behavior.

It is important to understand that most owners of aggressive (and even dangerous) dogs are like the parents of juvenile delinquents. They hate the problem but love the child. Complicating their lives are complaints, arguments, threats, and lawsuits from friends, relatives, neighbors, and lawful strangers. Utility workers refuse to enter their property. Letter carriers will not deliver their mail. Delivery people will not deliver. This is how it is when you live with dogs that bite, bark, lunge, chase, threaten, bully, growl, or rush or sneak up on anyone entering their territory. Such pet owners are in an emotional pickle and aren't sure where to turn or what to do. Do not despair — help is on the way.

Although some misguided folks want aggressive dogs (presumably for protection), most do not. Making a dog aggressive is like leaving a loaded gun lying on the carpet. Sooner or later a tragedy will occur because no one can predict or control such a dog's behavior. Protection dogs are totally obedient animals who have gone through specialized training from highly skilled professionals. However, millions upon millions of dogs are simply pets who are members of the families they live with. They are companion animals who have the most important job of making people feel needed, loved, and less alone. Living with a dog should be fun, especially for children and other smart people.

As head of the National Institute of Dog Training in Los Angeles, co-author Matthew Margolis has had many people come to him with great concern about their dogs' aggressive-behavior problems. They all experience great anxiety over this problem. A staggering 80 percent of his clientele seek help for aggressive-behavior problems. A large number of dogs in his training kennel are there undergoing aspects of behavior modification, training, and retraining, in an effort to make them easier to live with and, in some cases, less dangerous.

The concentration of media attention on dog attacks

and the fear of such attacks has had a profound effect on the public's attitude toward dogs in general and Pit Bulls (and other breeds perceived to be dangerous) in particular.

The sensational stories in newspapers and on TV news about dogs that have attacked people indicate how upset and impatient communities are becoming with those who keep aggressive dogs and continue to make excuses for them. *GRRR!* hopes to fill an important gap in pet-owner literature, one that relates to aggressive dog behavior in a useful, helpful way. The idea is to educate pet owners and help them prevent and remedy (where possible) the disturbing problem of aggressive dog behavior.

Pet owners must acknowledge and learn to cope with their dogs' aggressive behavior. Well-informed dog owners can make an important contribution to finding a solution to this serious problem by refusing to accept such behavior as permanent or hopeless.

We believe that dog owners can help themselves by learning how to select a dog for its good temperament and also by learning how to prevent aggressive behavior from developing into serious problems. By knowing the early signs of aggressive behavior and how to correct it properly, pet owners are likely to prevent it from becoming dangerous.

What if the troubled dog owner already lives with an aggressive dog that is scaring him and everyone else? Well, some dogs can be changed completely, some can be made manageable, and some, unfortunately, cannot be changed at all. That's the truth of the matter. If a dog is dangerously aggressive and cannot be changed, it is better to know that. Offered here is essential information about canine aggressive behavior along with some remedies for behavioral change where possible and various preventive methods and techniques. *GRRR!* offers what is possible.

We wish to applaud those who own dogs with aggressive-behavior problems who are willing to address the issues and for their valiant efforts to solve their problems. In doing so they are being good neighbors, good citizens, and great dog owners. Bravo!

# GRRR!

# 1

## Is Your Dog Aggressive?

*Love me, love my dog!* This is a sentiment that we seldom hear expressed anymore, despite the fact that many people continue to feel it deeply. Dogs are our favorite pets because they can blend instantly with any family or simply create a family where there was none before. Although they are frequently bought for children, few adults can resist the unrestrained happiness of a dog whose greatest joy is to be in the company of humans. The problem is that not all dogs are friendly to all humans. As a matter of fact, many pet owners have discovered that their dogs can be quite aggressive, hostile, or even dangerous, and they do not know what to do about it.

Nevertheless, there isn't a dog alive — even the most aggressive — that cannot capture the heart of at least one human being. Most people love most dogs, even those that are too aggressive. The reasons are understandable.

There is no such thing as a perfect dog. However, there

are important positive qualities to look for when considering a new dog or evaluating your family pet. An enjoyable dog is one that is happy, outgoing, loving, social, playful, and very friendly. The dog you choose to live with should be the most loving puppy or adult in the world. He should not be shy with people or seriously frightened of new areas or noises. If he hides behind people or furniture or runs away from you, he is seriously shy or frightened. You should be able to touch a dog all over — on every part of the body — without getting an aggressive or terrified reaction.

If you already have a dog and are planning to get another, make sure your second dog is of the opposite sex. This will practically guarantee no fighting between them. If you get a second dog, do not put the two dogs together right away. First, introduce them on neutral territory, in a park or in another part of your neighborhood. Do not introduce them inside or outside your house. Keep them apart for at least two weeks if possible, so that the new puppy has the opportunity to bond with the family. This is very important. Otherwise, the new dog will bond to the senior dog rather than to the family. This is likely to create a shy or aggressive dog that is not attached to human family members in a loving way. If you cannot keep them completely apart for the first two weeks, then try to keep the puppy away from the senior dog for at least six to eight hours a day, giving him exclusive time with the family.

It is a mistake to acquire two dogs at the same time. Wait at least six months to a year between dogs. Every dog needs individual attention, which is impossible to give two new dogs at the same time. One will become shy and the other aggressive. Pet dogs need humans more than they need each other.

Getting a dog and learning to live with him is a major event and an exciting addition to anyone's life. Within minutes after his arrival, a dog becomes part of the family and manages to burrow into the hearts of everyone he meets. The dog is a four-legged relative who plays a unique role in the human environment as friend, companion, worker, and, in some homes, protector. A dog is an endearing confidant who always listens and gives the best advice, which is to give no advice at all. A dog is one of the few constants a person can count on in an unpredictable, ever-changing world. Consequently, we humans develop strong feelings for our dogs and tend to forgive all of their faults and are often blind to them.

Some people demand protection from their dogs and do everything they can to encourage them to be unfriendly and threatening, especially to strangers. These are misguided people. They consider their dog's intimidating behavior toward anyone outside their family to be a good thing. Unfortunately, these dog owners rarely understand the difference between protection and uncontrolled aggression. Anyone who loves dogs should learn what the difference is between a protection dog and a dog that is simply aggressive.

A protection dog is a highly trained animal that responds without question to the commands of its handlers. Professional protection trainers teach dogs to defend their owners and their property and to accept the control of their owners or handlers. A trained protection dog knows what is expected of him and, most important of all, is a totally obedient animal. By contrast, an aggressive dog is a dangerous animal because he is unpredictable and uncontrollable.

Aggressive behavior in dogs is most often inherited and can be seen early in the animal's life, while he is still a puppy. Such puppies are all too often brought into the world by careless, ignorant, or inhumane breeders, whose only motivation is profit and who haven't the slightest idea or concern about the harm they do.

The lack of proper socialization by this type of breeder during the critical stages of puppyhood has a profound influence on a dog's behavior as an adult. The best you can hope for from an unsocialized dog is a pet that is less adaptive to human handling but somewhat manageable. At worst, an unsocialized dog may become highly aggressive and dangerous. Socialization is a process of human handling in a gentle, loving manner from the third to the sixteenth week of puppyhood.

Aggressive behavior can also be the result of a constantly hostile or threatening environment in any period of a dog's life. Dogs trying to survive on their own may become aggressive or fearful because of the need to defend themselves or to fight for food or shelter. Aggressive behavior is most often the response to physical abuse. Harsh punishments, abusive training techniques, and all forms of negative human behavior almost always create aggressive behavior in dogs.

Foolish people who deliberately antagonize their dogs in order to make them protective frequently create permanent, uncontrollable aggressive behavior. They encourage or teach their dogs to bark at strangers, growl at strangers, or attack strangers. The problem is that there are 250 million strangers out there, and most of them are law-abiding citizens. Everyone is a stranger to such dogs, and without an introduction from the owner, they will threaten, chase, or attack them. Dogs such as these bark and bite indiscriminately. People who tolerate or encourage canine aggression and do nothing to change this behavior will eventually be liable for dog-bite injuries. This always results in legal problems, medical bills, and considerable emotional stress. All that is in addition to the moral questions involved when a dog owner's negligence causes harm to an innocent person.

Of course biting is not the only form of aggressive behavior in dogs. When a dog chases joggers, walkers, stray animals, cars, bicycles, rollerbladers, and others, he is being aggressive. Barking that is intense and menacing is another form of aggressiveness whether it is from inside a car or behind a fence. Territorial marking (urinating or defecating) indoors as an assertion of dominance is aggressive. Pulling on a leash, jumping on people, nipping, mouthing, jumping on or over fences, running out the door, exhibiting sexual behaviors toward humans, and various other actions and responses are all aspects of aggressive behavior. These actions can be dangerous, frightening, or upsetting, depending on the circumstances and the degree of intensity. Making matters worse is the possibility that the dog may bite someone who attempts to stop his aggressive behavior.

The first and foremost step in solving an aggressive-behavior problem is getting past the stage of denial and admitting that a problem exists. Because most dog owners love their dogs as though they were their children, they overlook and forgive almost any form of negative behavior, no matter how upsetting or dangerous it is for themselves or others. But dog owners must learn to recognize and acknowledge their pets' aggressive behavior. This is essential if the behavior is going to be changed or brought under control. The first steps to dealing with the problem are to stop denying it exists and to stop making excuses.

Dog owners must learn how to identify aggressive behavior, whether it is observed in a puppy, juvenile, or fully mature dog, so that the proper action can be taken. By doing so, they may prevent the problem from becoming permanent or learn how to reduce it where it already exists. Here, then, is a definition that can help anyone determine if they have an aggressive dog: *Aggressive behavior in dogs, no matter what their size, type, or age, involves threatening actions and responses, especially growling, snarling, and snapping as a warning or actual attempt to cause physical injury.*

It is important to understand that when a dog is aggressive, the issue is *control,* and he will do anything to get it. Aggressive behavior is a means to an end, with only a few exceptions.

When a dog barks, it can be an uninhibited response to the presence of a stranger or a serious warning to an intruder. Barking can also be a response to another dog, an expression of excitement, loneliness, or boredom. It can also be a bad habit with no cause at all. However, when a dog growls or snarls and bares its teeth, it is a threat to a person or another dog. What could follow is a warning snap of the front teeth, a superficial bite, one or more painful bites, or a furious attack, knocking the victim to the ground with a rapid onslaught of harmful bites. Few dog owners are capable of stopping this behavior before serious injuries are incurred. Everyone should understand that an aggressive dog might very well chase or attack innocent children or adults who enter his territory. The truth is that an aggressive dog has more control over his owner and himself than anyone would like to admit.

Drawing on our extensive experience with aggressive dogs, we have classified aggressive-dog behavior according to ten categories. We hope this will make it easier to understand and work with the specific problems whether you are a professional or nonprofessional dog person. Within each category, we provide our own descriptions of the behavior, when it happens, and what we think causes it. To better illustrate some of these categories we provide a few case studies of actual aggressive-dog problems experienced by clients of the National Institute of Dog Training in Los Angeles. In these composites of various case histories, we describe the dog, his family and environment, his type of aggression, the techniques used to solve the problem, and the result.

It is essential to understand that a dog's behavior can reveal any combination of these ten categories of aggression. In some extreme cases, he may even exhibit all ten. Which category or categories of aggressive behavior a dog exhibits depends on whether he has a dominant aggression or fear aggression. For example, a dog can be territorial-aggressive in his backyard, in his car, in his home, and next to his owner or the front door, all of which are associated with dominant aggression. But the same dog can also be fear-aggressive when he is not in his own territory, where he feels safe. Some dogs are possessive-aggressive over food, toys, people, even with their family, but become shy or fear-aggressive with strangers. Sometimes the reverse is true, where a dog is shy and submissive with his family but aggressive with strangers. Do not leap to conclusions regarding your dog's type of aggressive behavior until you have given him the personality tests in chapter 3, "How Aggressive *Is* Your Dog? Tests and Signs of Aggression." The results will influence which training techniques to use in chapter 4, "How to Obedience-Train an Aggressive Dog." It can be counterproductive or even dangerous to misread your dog's aggressive behavior and let your guard down. You must always assume he can growl or bite over one or more of the aggressive-behavior categories listed below:

1. Dominant Aggression
2. Fear Aggression
3. Territorial/Overprotective Aggression
4. Possessive Aggression
5. Punishment Aggression
6. Pain Aggression
7. Predatory Aggression
8. Maternal Aggression
9. Dogfighting Aggression
10. Redirected Aggression

## Dominant Aggression

### Description

Although a dominant dog is usually a friendly dog with an assertive personality, a dominant-aggressive dog is an overbearing bully. Such dogs are overconfident and tend to behave like tyrants. Their goal is to be the top dog in all situations, especially within their own families. They may bark, growl, bare their teeth, snap, or bite to prove a point or get their way. A dominant-aggressive dog may try

to intimidate some family members but not all. Usually only one or two members of the family have any control over such a dog. He will always bully the least assertive person and dominate children. Dominant-aggressive dogs are usually aggressive with their families, but they are a threat mostly to strangers.

The problem with a dominant-aggressive dog is his inability to understand which strangers entering his territory should be allowed to do so and which should not. At times he may act friendly toward strangers but suddenly turn aggressive.

The body language of a dominant-aggressive dog involves his attempt to look as large and as threatening as he can. He may turn sideways to look more imposing as the hairs (or hackles) running along his spine rise and stand away from the body. He may also stand sideways to block your path. His tail and ears may rise straight up as his body posture becomes rigid and tense. Ironically, his tail may wag, creating the false impression that he is playful.

Facial expressions may vary from friendly to stern with a serious stare or bared teeth. The dog's stance indicates there is no possibility of backing off. The body language of a dominant-aggressive dog indicates a lack of submissiveness. The most threatening aspect of aggressive body language is direct eye contact. When a human or other dog stares back for a short length of time, the dominant-aggressive dog feels challenged and may attack.

## When It Occurs

The signs of dominant aggression are present in dogs as young as three months but are most apparent from ten months to three years. Male dogs are more likely to exhibit this form of aggressiveness, but it is also present in some females.

A dominant-aggressive dog may become threatening or dangerous when he rolls over on his back or when he is petted, groomed, or has his stomach rubbed as a puppy. This may also happen when a human stands over him as a puppy or an adult when he is lying down, when he is awakened from a sound sleep, or when he is pushed out of the way because he is blocking someone's path. He may also become nasty when anyone goes near his food, toys, or other possessions.

This behavior may also be seen when anyone tries to move him off a bed or a sofa. The dog will definitely react in a threatening manner when he feels challenged in a physical or overbearing way, such as being slapped or hit in any way as punishment for house soiling, chewing, digging, or any other unacceptable behavior. People can provoke threatening behavior by pointing at the dog in anger, scolding him harshly, threatening him physically, attempting to get a leash and collar in place, or by standing over a human on the floor, especially a child. From the point of view of a dominant-aggressive dog, anyone crossing his path or entering his territory without the owner's consent runs the risk of an aggressive response. To such dogs their territory can extend to the family car, a bed, a sofa, the kitchen floor, food (his or yours), or a specific member of his family.

## Reasons for This Behavior

**Genetics.** Dominant aggression is almost always inherited. One or both of the dog's parents are likely to have been dominant-aggressive dogs, passing this behavior on to their puppies through the genes. A dog's dominant-aggressive behavior may also be the result of a combination of inherited behavior, unusually high levels of testosterone (male hormones) circulating throughout the body, learned behaviors from other dogs, and as a response to abusive treatment and harsh living conditions.

**Human Behavior.** Aggressive behavior in dogs is often the result of a lack of socialization and being isolated in a yard or dog run. Without the opportunity to make friends with people outside the family or with other dogs, a dog will inevitably become distrustful and aggressive. Other negative human influences involve failing to correct dogs for their aggressive behavior, especially as puppies, or allowing them to dominate the household. Some people encourage their dogs to be dominant by allowing or rewarding aggressive behavior. Some dog owners foolishly believe that dominant-aggressive behavior is desirable. They consider their pets to be protective watchdogs when in fact they are merely dangerous, aggressive dogs that cannot be controlled. Another important and common influence on this behavior is families that allow or encourage their dogs to be the pack leaders of their households. This occurs when the dog is not disciplined for unacceptable behavior and is allowed to decide for himself who is permitted to enter their property and who is not. Such a dog not only dominates all situations but appears to run the household as though he were the leader of the pack. It is unworkable and inappropriate for a dog to determine how his human family must live.

## PEBBLES

Bonnie Jordan was a lawyer living in a small, charming house on one of those sunny Los Angeles streets that are as clean and shiny as a Mercedes showroom. She was a professional whose new young dog had so deeply gotten under her skin that she could no longer imagine life without him. After putting in a tough day in criminal court, she required bare feet, a cool drink, and quality time with her new dog. Heaven is a warm hug with a furry tail. Attach a cool nose to it and you are in puppy paradise. But the day she called Matthew at his training kennel it was paradise lost.

She sounded frantic on the phone, as she became another distraught dog owner calling for help. "Mr. Margolis, I'm Bonnie Jordan, and I am scared of my puppy." Matthew asked her what the problem was, and she said that he had recently started growling at her whenever she played with him. "What type of growl is it?" asked Matthew. "Is it a playful growl, or do you think it's a vicious growl?" She answered, "It sure isn't playful. He just utters this low growl from his throat and looks me straight in the eyes and takes on a kind of scary stance." What she described was very aggressive behavior.

Matthew asked her what kind of dog she had, and she immediately softened her voice. She answered lovingly, "He's a Cardigan Welsh Corgi. You know, the one with the tail." "What's his name?" "Pebbles," she cooed. "Well, there's your problem right there. Change his name," said Matthew, trying to lighten the conversation. She didn't think it was funny. He knew he wasn't going to console her that way so he got down to business and asked her questions about Pebbles's personality. He explained to her that most dominant dogs are fearless, and as they get older can be quite aggressive. But they can also be very loving, he quickly added. They believe they are leader of the pack and top dog of the family.

Bonnie confessed to Matthew that Pebbles was somewhat shy with new people, especially men. He asked if she lived alone and whether the dog saw many new people. He knew the answer even before she gave it. Of course he didn't. She revealed that the dog had often acted in a fearful way, with a sort of Jekyll-and-Hyde personality. At times he was afraid, and other times he was aggressive.

Matthew asked how the dog was outside with noises or bikes or things fast moving. She said kids on bikes would startle Pebbles, but he would get over it quickly and chase them.

Matthew then proceeded to get some background information on the dog. Bonnie told him that she had decided on a Corgi after going to a lot of dog shows. She purchased Pebbles from a breeder who had an ad in the newspaper. Matthew asked her why she had wanted a Corgi, and she answered, "I wanted a big dog in a small body." Matthew pointed out to her that the breed was originally meant to herd sheep and cattle and that they were tough little dogs that controlled their herds by nipping at the backs of their feet.

Pebbles had become a force to be reckoned with. Bonnie was very worried. She was a first-time puppy owner and had no experience with a dog that growled at her, and the thought of giving him up was too unhappy for words. She loved him. She told Matthew that the situation was affecting her work. She was not defending her clients as well as she should because she was feeling so stressed. Matthew told her that this sometimes happens because of the personality of the dog. "Pebbles sounds like a very domi-

**Is Your Dog Aggressive?**

nant dog to me," said Matthew. He recommended a home visit for a consultation and made an appointment.

Matthew went to Bonnie's home, and as he knocked on the door he heard frantic scratching on it. As the door opened he looked down to see an eighteen-pound terror jumping all over. The first thing Matthew did was give the dog a personality test, which included tests for aggression. The results were interesting. The dog was sweet, responsive, a little shy. In addition, he had what Matthew considered "a real attitude problem." He told Bonnie that the dog wasn't that bad and that his behavior could be changed primarily by having him obedience-trained. To his surprise, Bonnie insisted on training her dog herself. Matthew told her that she would definitely be successful if she followed his advice. She must obedience-train her dog fully by teaching him to heel on a leash, to automatically sit when she stopped, to obey the commands "Sit" and "Sit-Stay," "Down" and "Down-Stay," and "Come When Called."

Bonnie asked, "Why do I have to do all that? I just want to stop him from growling." Matthew smiled and answered, "You must take and maintain absolute control of the dog and make sure that you are in charge. From now on, you must be the top dog. Your dog has to listen to you. All of these commands are very functional in your everyday life. By having the ability to execute these commands with Pebbles responding to you, you will have control over the dog." He told her she had to learn how to give proper leash correction, the "Corrective Jerk," which must be accompanied with the proper tone of voice. She said, "I don't know if I can be that firm." Matthew shook his head and said, "You told me that you're five foot one, one hundred ten pounds, physically fit. That you lift weights and run five miles a day. If you can do all those things, I imagine you can be quite firm. My guess is that you're not a pussycat when you go to court." She grinned. "But he's my baby. I don't want to be cruel to my doggie."

Matthew explained to her that teaching her dog obedience commands and using proper corrective techniques along with socializing him would give her the control she needed to stop all the growling and posturing. Of course it meant introducing the dog to a lot more people, going to more places, such as parks and malls, and exposing Pebbles to the outside world. These things would resolve Pebbles's aggressive problem as well as give Bonnie a beautifully trained and socialized dog.

On her oath as an officer of the court she promised that she would get started right away and keep at it until the dog was trained. Matthew told her he would look in on them after the first month to check on Bonnie's progress with Pebbles. It was a wonderful surprise for Matthew at the end of the first month to discover that Bonnie Jordan was true to her word. She was a very diligent dog owner. She corrected Pebbles properly whenever he growled or behaved aggressively and trained him on a daily basis. She decided that she was the top dog in the family. She also decided that if Pebbles was going to listen to her, then she had to be the teacher and he had to be the student. Matthew was impressed to see them walk beautifully together and to watch the dog "Sit" and then "Stay" on command.

Matthew told Bonnie to keep up the good work and to call him in about two months to let him know the outcome. Two months later, he received a phone call from Bonnie, who was bubbling with joy. She told him that Pebbles was a new person. "He listens to me, and he doesn't growl anymore." She told him how grateful she was that Matthew got her to train her dog despite Pebble's young age. Even though Pebbles was a dominant dog with a strong-willed personality who exhibited aggressive behavior, his owner was able to establish the control that she needed with training and corrective techniques. As Pebbles became much less aggressive, Bonnie Jordan became much more aggressive — in the courtroom of course. And they lived happily ever after.

## Fear Aggression

### Description

Most dog bites are the result of this form of aggression. Fear-aggressive dogs seem to be frightened most of the time. Their response to the people or events that scare them is to bark, growl, bare their teeth, snap, bite, or exhibit any combination of these behaviors. Some fear-

aggressive dogs will bark at the slightest disturbance, such as the doorbell, the telephone, an approaching visitor, an outside noise, or the sight or sound of a passerby. Such dogs are nervous and insecure. They tend to protect *themselves* rather than their owners. Of significant importance is the fact that fear-aggressive dogs may be large or small.

The body language of fear-aggressive dogs gives the impression of submission when in fact it indicates fear that will quickly turn to aggression. The ears of such dogs may draw back as their tails go down, rigidly tucked between their legs. They will avoid direct eye contact, cower, sidle away, or hide under a table or behind a sofa. This behavior is seen when they feel threatened by specific people (adults or children), other dogs (or cats), new places, or even some noises. Fear-aggressive dogs often shiver with fright, retreat, and run away. When they are cornered, they may growl and then bite. All their aggressive behavior stems from a defensive posture, including chasing after people once they turn their backs on them. When people run away from fear-aggressive dogs because they are frightened, they trigger hunting instincts in the dog that result in an upsetting chase.

An important aspect of this category of aggression develops as the dog begins to mature. The fearful, backing away behaviors change sometime between one and three years of age. At this stage the dog becomes bolder and seemingly less fearful. The fear aggression tends to combine with territorial aggression, which consequently makes these dogs more likely to attack. *Fear aggression at this stage accounts for the greatest number of biting incidents.* The age factor is an important aspect of accurately identifying fear aggression. A nine-month-old puppy will back away as it growls at you. A two-year-old fear-aggressive dog is more likely to lunge at you.

## When It Occurs

Dogs of this type exhibit fear-aggressive behavior when they feel threatened by the approach of strangers. They are most likely to exhibit this behavior in their homes or territories, where they feel the most secure; in enclosed areas, such as the inside of cars; while standing next to their owners in the yard, on a bed, or even while out for a walk. Fear-aggressive dogs bark, growl, or bite when approached as they cower under a table or a chair or wherever they feel trapped or cornered.

They usually respond aggressively when they are punished for such behavior problems as excessive barking, house soiling, or destructive chewing. When fear-aggressive dogs feel threatened, they either run away or stand their ground, ready to bite (the "fight-or-flight" response), depending on the circumstance. If they cannot escape they become dangerous.

Using your hands to point at your dog in anger, or threatening him with a rolled-up newspaper, or slapping the paper against your hand for effect, or actually hitting the dog while hollering at him only worsens the problem. A rolled-up newspaper is perceived by the dog as an extension of your arm. If you use your arm to punish the dog, he then becomes fearful of your arm or your hand, even when it is used to express love and affection. As you attempt to pet your dog after using your arms negatively, he is likely to cower. This reaction is based on the conditioning *you* have created. The dog now and forever associates your arm and your hands with fear or pain.

When fear-aggressive dogs are reprimanded harshly, they react by cowering, running away, or snapping and biting at the same time. Consider the difference in size between a human and a dog. To most dogs humans are towering giants. The human voice can also be overpowering in tone and volume. You must take into account a dog's hearing mechanism, which is far more sensitive than that of the human ear. The combination of a human's loud, powerful-sounding voice and exaggerated physical actions cause fear-aggressive dogs to become overwhelmed and overpowered, which almost always elicits aggressive behavior. Consequently, dogs in this situation may associate all human behaviors, including the mere presence of some people, as threatening.

## Reasons for This Behavior

**Genetics.** Many professionals working with dogs believe that most fear-aggressive dogs have inherited this temperament type and have the potential for all of the behavior problems connected with it. This conclusion is based on years of experience and observation. Another possibility is that fear-aggressive behavior is genetic in origin but requires external influences to elicit it.

**Human behavior.** This unpleasant, dangerous behavior develops when a pet dog has not been allowed to socialize with people or other dogs. As social animals, dogs must be allowed to interact with other people if they are to be secure, trustful pets. Some fear-aggressive dogs are shy with men (if they've been raised by women); shy with women (if they've been raised by men); or shy with children (if they've been raised without children). Seeing an occasional child in the neighborhood is not the same as being raised with one or more on a daily basis.

An important cause of the development of fear aggression is making a dog overprotective by encouraging him to be unfriendly and suspicious of strangers. Another cause is responding with harsh verbal or physical reprimands when a dog displays aggressive behavior. This can cause him to bark or growl out of fear, which compounds the fear and aggressive behavior.

When a dog owner says, "Okay. It's okay," as his dog barks or growls (out of fear), he is actually rewarding the aggressive behavior with a positive reinforcement. The owner thinks he is telling his dog that the person he is growling at is okay. But the dog misinterprets this as a confirmation that he is doing the right thing. Few owners understand that they are actually teaching the dog to bark and growl. This represents a major communication problem between dogs and their owners.

**Environmental Influences.** Dogs that are raised in a yard and never allowed to relate to anyone but their immediate families usually become fear-aggressive animals. As these dogs get older, they become very territorial and even more aggressive than before.

Fear aggression can also develop if a dog is raised in a kennel too long before finding another home. Purchasing a puppy and removing him from his kennel environment by approximately seven to eight weeks of age is an important aspect of his development. If a puppy is with his littermates at his critical stage of development, beyond four months of age, he may not be as adaptive to people as he is with other dogs. Such puppies appear to be outgoing in the kennel with their littermates. New dog owners, therefore, do not realize that the puppy of choice may be people-shy until they take him home. Personality testing is the best method for selecting the right puppy. See chapter 3, "How Aggressive *Is* Your Dog? Tests and Signs of Aggression."

Fear aggression can also develop when there are too many puppies in a litter and there is intense competition among them for warmth and mother's milk. It is not uncommon for one or more pups in a litter to fail to get enough nourishment, motherly attention, or human handling. Other causes of fear aggression in the litter are excessive bullying by littermates or not being socialized properly by the breeder or being taken away from the mother too soon (see "Socialization," in chapter 2, "How Did He Get That Way?"). Quite often the runt of the litter, alone and forced away from the food by the others, grows up to be a fear-aggressive dog that can be dangerous and difficult to live with.

## DEMPSTER

Sara Billings and Barney Hickman lived together with the idea of getting married the minute they could afford their own home. Part of their dream was to have a ready-made family by getting the perfect puppy. They wanted a big, huggy bear of a dog and decided on a Great Dane. After researching the breed, they went to see their first dog. There was only one puppy left, but it was love at first leap into their arms for the eleven-week-old puppy who was all legs and energy. They couldn't resist him and took the gangling dog home with them within the hour. Everything they had read so carefully about choosing a puppy went right out the window.

The young, hard-working couple shared a house with several of their friends, two of whom had dogs. So there they were under one roof, five hu-mans and three dogs. Because their new Great Dane puppy, now named Dempster, was "just a baby," they kept him locked in their bedroom during the entire day to keep him out of trouble while they were at their jobs. The young dog did not get out of the room until they came home, when he became the object of Sara's total attention. Dempster had become her child and was totally babied by her after a ten-hour absence each day. The growing dog went from a lonely state of isolation with no one to relate to him to one of excessive attention and over-stimulation.

Throughout Dempster's puppyhood most of his human contact was with Sara, who fed him, walked him, played with him, and held him and hugged him constantly. Barney played a minor role in the dog's life and accepted that position, like so many fathers with their children. As the months passed, Dempster began showing some of his

**Is Your Dog Aggressive?**

fear-aggression tendencies by yipping hysterically whenever he was startled or picked up. This was not taken seriously and considered somewhat amusing and, unfortunately, not recognized as the beginning of fear-aggressive behavior. Intensifying the dog's problems were punishments administered for destructive chewing (caused by teething), which is a normal problem for an adolescent dog. Barney would lose his temper and either yell at the young dog or spank him, depending on the severity of the damage to their possessions.

The first serious incident took place just before Dempster's first birthday. By then he was allowed the run of the house and the backyard. He was outside with the other two dogs that shared the house and had become his playmates. A large bag of dog food was left in the yard by mistake and the dogs began competing for it. The competition turned into a loud, dangerous dogfight, with Dempster injuring the other dogs. Luckily, Barney was home and able to break it up before it became ugly. From then on, the dogs were permanently separated for fear of Dempster's size and strength. Soon afterward Sara and Barney were finally able to rent a house of their own and moved out.

Moving brought with it a new problem. Whenever Dempster was left in the yard he barked without stopping at anyone who approached their house. Because of the complaints of their neighbors, Sara and Barney had to keep him indoors during the day when they were at work. Soon afterward, he began growling at Sara whenever she approached his toys and assorted possessions. Other problems developed. The large dog began shying away from anyone he didn't know and growled at them as they came near him or his house. He would bark and back away and hide behind Sara whenever he was confronted with anyone not part of his family. Dempster seemed to be more frightened of men than women and cowered at the sight of them.

The most serious incident to occur involved Sara's cousin, who was a houseguest for several days. Dempster dragged a blanket off the bed with his teeth and unexpectedly tossed it on the young woman's lap. When she tried to remove it, the full-grown Great Dane growled furiously and stood in front of her, staring in a threatening manner. From then on, Sara's cousin was very frightened of the dog and would not come back for a visit. That was the incident that motivated them to get help. They found Matthew and went for an evaluation.

After an extensive interview and several behavioral tests, Matthew concluded that Dempster was a fear-aggressive dog who had been insecure and shy as a puppy. He had bonded with the woman of the house because she exclusively raised him and babied him to the point that he could do anything he wanted with no corrections. Matthew prescribed six to eight weeks in his kennel, where the dog would be socialized and obedience-trained.

Dempster's reconditioning began with socialization. From the beginning he was exposed to many different people who were responsible for everything pertaining to his well-being, which included feeding, cleaning his space, grooming, training, and so on. His first training lesson involved getting him out of his dog run. The 140-pound dog did not want to cooperate and, due to his change of environment, became fearful whenever they tried to get him out. Matthew determined that his first trainer should be a woman. She began by talking gently and reassuringly to him in order to establish a bond of trust between them. She slowly and patiently convinced him to walk to the gate at the front of the run.

Once this bond was established it was soon transferred to the others who dealt with him on a daily basis.

When he was a puppy Dempster had been punished by being grabbed by the scruff of his neck and dragged from "the scene of his crimes." Having his neck touched had become associated with pain and severe reprimands. This made him extremely aggressive whenever his trainer tried to get a leash and collar around him. At first a lasso-type leash was tossed over his head from a distance, which gave the trainer control. Once he accepted the leash and collar, Dempster became much more cooperative and responsive to the teaching process. The dog progressed quickly.

Feeding Dempster was another problem in the beginning. He would not allow anyone to place his food down in front of him. He was extremely territorial and possessive. However, because of the ongoing obedience-training, his handlers were able to command him to stand back as they placed his food on the ground without fear of his lunging at them. He obeyed.

As the weeks passed, he developed confidence in himself and in his trainer. Matthew observed that the dog had adjusted well to the socializing

**Is Your Dog Aggressive?**

and training techniques and was ready for the next step, which was to work with another trainer, this time a man. At first Dempster became very upset and howled and hollered all the way from his run to the training area. Once he was given training commands, however, he responded properly and obeyed. He was becoming less fearful of men and more tolerant of most strangers. The large dog had also become more adaptive to new and different situations.

After eight weeks of intensive socialization and training, he was sent home, where his training continued with a once-a-week visit. Both owners were taught how to execute the train-ing commands and worked with the dog successfully, establishing the proper dominance over him. He was taken into new and different situations outside his home, where he was continually being socialized.

Although he was still territorial and possessive, he had improved enormously. He was allowed to have his toys only if a game of fetch was on the agenda, which forced him to relinquish the objects on command. With a new set of rules to live by and a new attitude about who was boss, Dempster was no longer the frightened dog he had been, and life became much more enjoyable than before. It was a happy ending.

## Territorial/Overprotective Aggression

### Description

The territorial/overprotective–aggressive dog barks threateningly at anyone entering his domain. He may growl, lunge, and even bite someone he considers a stranger or an intruder. Such a dog may claim the yard, the family car, a sofa, or one room in the house or the entire house. A territorially aggressive dog may even claim the area where his owners are standing on the street. This behavior may vary with different members of his family. His aggressiveness may also be a response to unexpected, intrusive sounds, such as the ringing of the doorbell or knocking at the door. Even the suggestion of an intruder

triggers the aggressive behavior. He may become aggressive while out for a walk when approached by a person who appears to be a stranger.

The dog's physical warning signs are clear. His body posture displays raised ears, a forward stance, a highly focused, intense facial expression, and an elevated tail (possibly wagging). The dog may bark or growl and may jump up and down.

The sudden motion of a stranger (even a child) will elicit predatory behavior, which involves chasing, knocking down, and possibly biting anyone running away from or toward him.

**Is Your Dog Aggressive?**

## When It Occurs

This form of aggression occurs when the dog reacts to a violation of his territory. He will threaten anyone who appears to be violating his space, which could be his yard, his house, his car, his personal possessions, including his sleeping space, or wherever his owner happens to be standing. He may protect his house by blocking the doorway or by chasing people away from his immediate surroundings. He is most likely to bite when a stranger, such as a letter carrier, meter reader, or delivery person, actually crosses the line and enters his domain.

This is especially true once the territorial/overprotective–aggressive dog has matured, which occurs between the ages of one and three years. Occasionally, a foolish but well-intentioned dog lover will place his or her hand in the open window of a car to pet a dog that is sitting inside. That person risks being bitten by any dog, but especially one that is highly territorial or overprotective. Such dogs also become aggressive when strangers go near their owners at home, in a veterinarian's office, or even on the street.

## Reasons for This Behavior

**Genetics.** Breeding has a great influence on the territorial/overpossessive–aggressive dog's behavior. If the parents were aggressive, in many cases the dog inherits their aggressive behavior.

Breeds such as the Akita and the Airedale have a tendency to be territorial-aggressive, along with a number of other breeds in the working, terrier, and sporting groups. A dog's natural protective tendencies come into play with breeds such as the German Shepherd Dog, Rottweiler, Chow Chow, and various others.

**Lack of Proper Socialization.** Keeping a dog away from most people, tying him up, continually confining him in a dog run, and never allowing him in the house are important causes of aggressive behavior of this type. When there is no interaction with people and other animals, the dog's natural territorial aggression becomes exaggerated. Territorial/overprotective aggression is often the result if the dog experiences little or no human contact and is encouraged to bark and growl because the owners want a guard dog.

The problem may also develop if there is more than one dog in the family, causing them to become socially dog-oriented rather than socially people-oriented, which is a serious problem. Dogs of this temperament may be shy with men (if raised by women), shy with women (if raised by men), or shy with children (if raised without children). It is important to understand that a dog who is raised with children in his neighborhood is not the same as a dog who is raised with children in his family. The children in his family are considered by him to be part of his pack and therefore accepted, defended, and often obeyed. Children who are not members of the family are usually regarded by such a dog as just smaller strangers and therefore not to be trusted or allowed into his territory.

**Environmental Influences.** Tying a dog to one place in the backyard and keeping him there most of the time brings with it the possibility of creating this form of aggressive behavior. In very short order his tiny bit of real estate becomes his entire world, creating in him the need to aggressively keep intruders away.

Aggressive behavior will also develop if passersby are allowed to go near the fence where the dog is confined and tease him or throw things at him or if lawnmowers and other engine-driven equipment designed to clean yards or swimming pools comes close by. These and other provocations can cause dogs to react aggressively.

**Dog Owners.** Encouragement from dog owners is a major reason for dogs behaving with territorial/overprotective aggression. Those who do this want their dogs to protect them but make the mistake of verbally and physically praising the dog when he barks or growls. It is impossible for dogs to distinguish when this behavior is appropriate or inappropriate. They cannot tell the good guys from the bad guys. This attitude is a major cause for the escalation of dangerous, aggressive canine behavior.

Certain games and types of play teach and encourage aggressive behavior. Games such as tug-of-war and wrestling on the floor tend to promote aggressive behavior in dogs. Tug-of-war teaches a dog to hold objects with his teeth, to shake them, and to bite them. As this takes place, he is praised and consequently rewarded for behavior that in another setting becomes dangerous. This is true for all dogs.

## Possessive Aggression

### Description

If a person or other pet goes near the dog's food or anything he considers to be his possession, the possessive-aggressive dog barks, growls, bares his teeth, snaps, or bites.

### When It Occurs

Approaching such a dog or getting close to his food bowl when he is being fed will set in motion his aggressive behavior. Touching him or attempting to take his playthings or any object he is involved with, such as a shoe, a towel, or a book, will cause him to growl or bite. There is no age limit for this behavior, and it is not gender specific. This form of aggressiveness may be seen in any dog or puppy, male or female. The older the dog, the more intense will be the aggression. A possessive-aggressive dog may become antagonistic because he regards a specific bed, chair, or even the floor where he is lying as his exclusive property.

## Reasons for This Behavior

**Survival Instinct.** Aggression based on possessiveness is rooted in a natural tendency to protect food from competitors within the litter or pack structure or from competing predators. As in the case of most canine behaviors, the need for such behavior in the human, dog-owning environment does not often exist. However, the instinct continues to influence behavior.

**Territory.** Because of abnormally exaggerated territorial instincts, possessive-aggressive dogs do not allow anyone to go near their possessions or their food.

**Dominance.** An overly dominant dog will behave aggressively when asserting his possession of specific objects, places, or persons.

**Other Reasons.** This behavior is sometimes found in abandoned or stray dogs that have experienced harshness. Another common reason for the development of this behavior is the owner's failure to correct the dog for aggressiveness, instead allowing it to continue from puppyhood into adulthood. Too often dog owners believe "puppies have a right to growl or snap" when their food or toys are taken away. Such dog owners irrationally identify with their dog's "feelings." There are dog owners who actually consider this potentially dangerous behavior to be amusing or cute and do all they can to encourage it.

## KEEFER

On a typical sunny day in Los Angeles a very pleasant couple drove to Matthew's training kennel with Keefer, their five-year-old Springer Spaniel, whom they jokingly called their son. They coasted into the driveway on an impulse to satisfy their curiosity about Matthew, whom they had seen on television a number of times. In a conversation with Matthew they raved about how well behaved Keefer was and what a good, loving dog he was . . . except for one slight behavior problem. He showed his teeth and threatened to bite them with a low, throaty growl if they tried to take something away from him. They didn't believe this was much of a behavior problem and had a casual attitude about it.

As they continued their discussion they also revealed that Keefer was not friendly with anyone outside his family. In order to demonstrate to the well-intentioned dog owners the seriousness of their dog's problem, Matthew placed a bowl of food on the floor for the chestnut-and-white spaniel. Keefer began to sniff at it. As Keefer examined the bowl, Matthew reached down and began to

take it away. As he did, the beautiful spaniel transformed from their "loving son" into a snarling, snapping demon displaying frightening and dangerous behavior. The young dog owners were shocked and somewhat heartbroken. As difficult as it was to accept, there was no way they could deny what they saw. They left the dog at Matthew's training kennel and signed a six-week commitment. They later told him that halfway home they turned around to retrieve the dog but thought better of it. They called the kennel they minute they got home to see how the dog was doing.

Matthew assured them the dog was fine, he was not suffering. As a matter of fact, he told them, Keefer was settling in well for a dog that had never been away from home. They were sure that in a couple of days they would need to pick him up because he would refuse to eat due to being separated from his family. But the dog ate well and didn't seem to mind his new accommodations one bit. Matthew told them, to their chagrin, that they were the ones suffering, not Keefer. The dog did well during his six weeks at "boot camp."

At first the dog stayed in the back of his individual run and watched all the trainers and handlers coming and going with other dogs. His own trainer convinced him that being taken out of the run (on a leash) was the only way to satisfy his curiosity about all the activity around him. Once he was taken to the front area of the kennel, where all the obedience-training took place, and saw all the familiar faces that talked to him, fed him, and groomed him, he seemed to relax. Obedience-training came easily for him because he was smart and a quick learner. Soon he began to look forward to going to the training area in order to perform. It was an upbeat, positive experience for him every time.

Once he learned the basic obedience commands, it was time to address the problem of releasing objects that were in his mouth. At first he reacted to the trainer's actions as a game. Once he understood the trainer was serious, Keefer's possessive-aggressive behavior reared its ugly head. He growled and bared his teeth with unmistakable menace. However, Keefer was in for a rude awakening. He did not get the reaction to which he had become accustomed. What he got was a sharp leash correction each and every time, and that surprised him, to say the least. His aggression was not met with fear, nor did it get him

what he wanted. Instead, he was reprimanded by those whose authority he had come to accept and thrive on. As the weeks passed, objects were set in front of him to admire but not touch. This was to teach him that things on the ground were not necessarily there for him. An obedience command was given if he so much as looked at the objects purposely set before him.

Once Keefer was able to walk by without paying any attention to what was on the ground, the trainer proceeded to the next step. Keefer was encouraged to select an object to play with and carry around in his mouth. However, on a "Drop" command, he was taught to drop the object and allow the trainer to pick it up. This was first done with two people so that no one would get bitten. One person focused on correcting the dog as the other one extracted the toy from his jaws. Keefer could hardly believe that anyone would try to take his prize away. Despite this, the minute a growl was heard he was corrected.

The trainer would tell the second handler to approach the dog and give the "Drop" command. If Keefer refused or hesitated to release the object, he was given another leash correction. Corrections depend on the size and type of dog and the degree of aggression that has to be managed. A spray bottle filled with water is all some dogs need to get the message while others require a firm leash-and-collar correction. The types of toys or objects used for this training are also important. A large toy may be necessary so that there is enough showing to safely hold on to without getting bitten. If your dog is very aggressive, over two years of age, and sixty pounds or more, consult a professional dog trainer before attempting to use the "Drop" command and the corrections described above. The consequences of a mistake could involve the loss of a hand.

Once Keefer understood that he was no longer in control, he started to give up the toys without protest. After each correction, he was given his reward, which consisted of verbal praise for doing a good job. His reward became much more important to him than the toys he left behind or dropped from his mouth. These techniques continued throughout his six-week stay at the kennel and needed to be carried through for the rest of his life. If Keefer were ever allowed the upper hand again, it would not take long for his possessive-aggressive be-

havior to start up all over again. His "parents" were amazed at his progress and, of course, thought he was the smartest dog in his class. On completion of his training they took him home. It was a beautiful day when they all left, and they gave Keefer a graduation party as soon as they got home.

It is important to understand that as Keefer was being trained, so were his owners. Along every step of the way his owners were taught how to execute each command and correction so that the dog would not merely behave properly with the trainer but with his owners, who were not only in charge but were, in effect, his trainers for the rest of his life.

Life was good. There were no more trainers, no more lessons. Wrong! The doorbell rang the following week, and there was his trainer from the kennel. Training was not finished. It continued in his home, in his territory, and even in his neighborhood. It all went well and Keefer's family was filled with pride and pleasure at their dog's new attitude and behavior. They could not talk about anything but the change in the dog as they all began to relax and enjoy their new lifestyle.

**Is Your Dog Aggressive?**

## Punishment Aggression

### Description

The dog barks (or talks back to its owners), growls, bares its teeth, snarls, and bites when being hit, yelled at, or overly dominated.

### When It Occurs

This form of aggression is aroused when people hit their dogs with their hands or rolled-up newspapers, chase them, or corner them, allowing no avenue of escape. Dogs in this predicament will respond aggressively to being hit as a form of punishment. The same is true when they are deliberately frightened as a reprimand for so-called bad behavior. Some people become enraged or frightened by their dog's aggressive behavior despite the fact that they are the cause of it by hitting or harshly scolding him.

## Reasons for This Behavior

The primary cause of punishment aggression is hitting, yelling, pointing at, or standing over a dog in a threatening manner. Many dogs will respond aggressively to threatening human body language in combination with verbal abuse and physical punishments. Some dog owners mistakenly punish their dogs for behavior problems, such as housebreaking mistakes, destructive chewing, or digging. This almost always provokes an aggressive or frightened response. Grabbing a dog by the scruff of the neck in anger creates aggression. Abusive handling, such as grabbing the dog by the jowls, holding his mouth closed, cuffing him under the chin, or using your hands in any other threatening manner can all result in dog bites. The same is true of abusive training techniques, such as grabbing, spanking, hitting, cuffing, or any other negative use of the hands. These not only create aggressive responses; they prevent dogs from accepting your hands for obedience training or expressions of affection. A punishment-aggressive dog will cringe when you try to pet him. Dogs that have been hit will literally bite the hand that feeds them.

### Pain Aggression

## Description

The dog growls, snaps, bites, or howls when touched on a pain-sensitive area of his body. Because some dogs are more tolerant of pain in specific areas of their bodies than others are, this form of aggressive behavior is not always apparent until it is too late. Some dogs have a high tolerance for pain, and many do not.

## When It Occurs

A dog may behave aggressively and bite if he is handled improperly when he is sick or injured. This may happen even when a member of his family is handling him. Pain-aggression behavior, however, is most often seen in dogs when they are being bathed, groomed, medicated, trained, or in the course of veterinary examinations. Even friendly gestures, such as petting or rubbing, can promote an aggressive reaction.

Grooming can hurt pain-aggressive dogs when they are combed or brushed too hard. This is most likely to happen if their coats are matted or tangled. Professional groomers and knowledgeable dog owners use a detangling liquid or coat conditioner to soften knotted areas of the fur. Despite this, a dog may howl even if he is touched gently in a pain-sensitive area.

Nail-clipping accidents are a common cause of continuing pain-aggressive responses. Some dogs respond aggressively to being bathed or to specific aspects of a bath, such as getting wet, being lathered with shampoo (per-

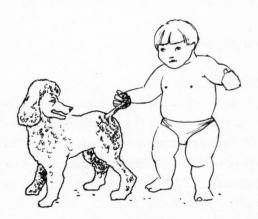

haps the soap burned his eyes), or being rinsed, toweled, or blow-dried.

## Reasons for This Behavior

**Genetics.** Pain sensitivity in specific areas of the body is frequently an inherited characteristic in puppies and dogs and if so, can be altered only by behavioral reconditioning.

**Medical Problems.** Many aggressive behaviors are merely involuntary reactions to the pain caused by a medical problem that may not be obvious, such as hip dysplasia, arthritis, bladder stones, skin disorders, ear problems, and various other problems. Any one of these will cause a dog to snap or bite when he is handled or even lightly touched. A dog cannot tell you he is in pain. His natural response to being touched in a painful area is either to run from you or to try to stop you from touching him by growling, snapping, or biting. These reactions are instinctive and do not allow the dog to consider that he may be biting the person who loves him the most. Medical conditions require professional diagnoses and therapies from a veterinarian. The obvious solution to this problem begins with addressing the possibility of a medical problem.

Medicating a dog in an area of the body where he may be in pain, such as the ears or the anus, could cause growling or snapping. Ears occasionally become infected or invaded by parasites, and anal glands may become impacted or infected, all of which will make these areas painful when touched.

As dogs get older they become less tolerant of pain because of failing health, frequent illness, arthritis, or simply the aging process itself. Older dogs can become cranky and intolerant of being handled to any great extent.

**Grooming.** A reaction to pain when being groomed is very common. Usually the professional groomer or dog owner is unaware of a dog's sensitive areas until he or she touches them. Of course, the improper use of grooming tools will also cause a pain-aggressive reaction. A dog's coat requires that it be maintained with specific grooming tools designed for its type, texture, and length. Using the wrong scissors, brushes, combs, electric clipper heads, or nail cutters will definitely hurt a sensitive dog, and he may express pain with his teeth.

## MARJ

Marj was a four-year-old with a classic, blunt-muzzle Boxer face. She had the chiseled features of a champion framed in a polished, mahogany coat that reflected its deep luster in natural light. A blaze of smooth white fur spread across her broad chest like a splash of silk. She was a beautiful, healthy dog in every way except for her infrequent and unexpected flashes of aggressiveness. She had bitten people on three separate occasions. She bit the lady of the house when she touched her ear; the man of the house as he tried to run a comb through her coat; and she bit a neighbor known to her for a long time, when he attempted to pet her through the fence.

The dog's family was a middle-aged couple with no children who had rescued her from an animal shelter at the age of three. After the first biting incident, they assumed she had been abused or hit in her previous life. For a while they thought they could change this behavior by treating her with kindness and understanding. As time passed they discovered that she didn't want to be touched and she didn't want certain people in her territory. This included various friends and relatives. Although Marj was for the most part a lovable dog, her owners noticed that she was not very sociable when away from her home.

After the third biting incident, it was clear that the situation was beyond their control and getting dangerous. They called Matthew and became clients after the initial interview and temperament tests. His first encounter with the dog was in the owners' car. Although Matthew approached the vehicle in a nonthreatening manner, the dog became extremely agitated and bared her teeth with a menacing snarl. There was no way to talk the dog out of the car or to get in without being attacked. On Matthew's instructions the lady of the house slid a leather leash and metal training collar around Marj's neck and then handed it to him. This gave him immediate control over the dog and he was able to open the door slowly and entice her to walk out on her own. She did this without incident.

After several simple behavior tests Matthew determined that one of Marj's biggest problems was that she had a very low tolerance for pain or the fear of pain. He felt this was probably the major source of her aggressive behavior. She was also excessively territorial. Once she was removed from the car, and the obligation to defend it, she mildly walked into the kennel area of Matthew's "summer camp" for training and reconditioning.

Because Marj seemed to respond better to women than to men, a woman trainer was assigned to her for the first part of her stay. Getting Marj out of her kennel run the first few times was touch-and-go until the dog accepted the trainer as a dominant person in her life. Obedience-training was the strongest link to making the situation safe for everyone involved. The dog was first taught to "Sit" and then "Sit-Stay." These commands were used extensively when getting the dog out of the run and returning her. She was expected to "Sit" and "Stay" as the gate was opened and the leash and collar were placed around her neck.

A release word was then used to signal that it was okay to move out of position. Once she accepted the routine, she was fairly happy about coming in and out of her run. At this point the training and the reconditioning process could get into full swing. Like most dogs, she

**Is Your Dog Aggressive?**

began to enjoy the training lessons and looked forward to them. They gave her a sense of accomplishment. She wanted to perform well and be rewarded with praise. She was like all other dogs. What she did not like was the daily inspection of her body and her weekly bath, which was an important part of the reconditioning process. It always involved a second person, who would touch her in various parts of her body while she was expected to stand still and accept this or be corrected by her trainer.

Reconditioning her aversion to being touched involved a slow, patient process of desensitization. This involved creating positive associations with the very thing the dog feared the most. It began by touching her in an area she feared the least, her left haunch, and only for a quick pat and a short rub. Lavish verbal praise and a tiny tidbit of cooked liver then followed it. This was continued through-out each day of Marj's stay at the kennel. As she became more tolerant of being touched, the trainer and the handler extended the process to her legs, her tail, her ears, her torso. By the fifth week of her stay, she was allowing a wide variety of trainers and handlers to touch her, pat her, and even pull on her coat and tail.

Once the six weeks were completed at the kennel, the training continued in Marj's home, where she learned to accept both family members as dominant. Home training consisted of teaching the dog the conventional obedience commands, such as "Sit," "Stay," "Heel," "Down," "Come When Called," and "Place." As she was taught basic obedience commands, her reconditioning for pain continued. Marj soon learned that she did not have the upper hand in her home and was expected to live with a new set of rules.

## Predatory Aggression

### Description

The dog barks, chases, nips, or bites people who are in motion.

### When It Occurs

Dogs with predatory aggression chase cars, bikes, motorcycles, or anything that moves quickly. Joggers, rollerbladers, and even those strolling by, who are not protected by the exterior of a vehicle, are very likely to be chased or bitten. Dogs such as these almost always chase after those who become frightened and run.

This form of aggression pertains to hunting or stalking prey. Some dogs hunt and others do not, but the instincts are present in all dogs to some degree. Once a prey animal is detected, the dog watches intensely, follows slowly, stalks with serious hunting behaviors, gives chase, and

**Is Your Dog Aggressive?**

then attacks as the target runs in fear. Dogs with predatory aggression will chase any variety of moving objects. Predatory dogs usually attack animals or people when they move away rather than when they approach.

## Reasons for This Behavior

This form of aggression represents an instinctive urge to hunt by stalking, chasing, and biting the quarry.

### Maternal Aggression

## Description

Maternal aggression is directed toward humans as well as animals and is characterized by barking, growling, snapping, and any behavior meant to discourage your presence. This behavior stops or at least diminishes dramatically once the mother's puppies are weaned. It usually stops entirely when the last of the litter is gone or off on its own as an adolescent dog.

## When It Occurs

This behavior is most frequently seen in a female nursing or rearing a litter of puppies. Aggressive behavior is aroused whenever anyone, human or animal, approaches her whelping area, nest, or her puppies.

## Reasons for This Behavior

Maternal aggression is essentially protective in nature. It is instinctive for all canine mothers to protect their young and guard their whelping areas.

## Dogfighting Aggression

### Description

Barking, growling, biting, lunging, chasing, and wrestling are the frightening behaviors displayed in a serious dogfight. Swift, twisting motions and frightening sounds of snarling growls and throaty howls of pain are characteristic of these terrible encounters. Dominance, fear, and territory are usually the issues involved. All of these behaviors can be seen in a form of rehearsal or learning in the play behavior of puppies but without the frightening threat of injury. And of course there is always a certain amount of aggressive behavior between dogs that is simply a part of play or investigative interaction that does not usually progress to a dogfight.

## When It Occurs

Most fighting occurs between dogs of the same sex. Males usually fight other males. Females usually fight other females. There are exceptions to this rule, however. Dogfighting behavior is triggered when one dog observes another in the distance as it approaches its territory. This will happen if the aggressive dog is in a yard, a car, standing next to its owner, on or off a leash. Aggression such as this can be instigated at home between dogs living together or between visiting dogs over the issues of territory, the intrusion of personal space, or possessions.

## Reasons for This Behavior

Dogs that fight are competitive and territorial, with the issue of dominance versus subordination as a primary focus. This form of behavior is often the result of little or no socializing during puppyhood. Young dogs living together may develop fighting behaviors over food, various possessions, and the attention of their owners.

Some dog owners, without knowing it, create this form of aggression by giving one dog more attention and affection than another. Aggressive behavior is often seen as one dog stands next to its owner receiving attention and is then approached by another dog in the family. The aggressive behavior is often interpreted as an expression of jealousy but is more accurately defined as competition for the owner's affection and attention. (Jealousy is a complex human reaction.) In this situation, with two dogs of the same sex, the owner should favor the most dominant dog to avoid aggressive behavior.

## Redirected Aggression

### Description

Dogs that show this form of behavior bark, growl, snap, or bite a person or animal that interrupts aggressive behavior that is focused elsewhere.

### When It Occurs

When a dog is about to fight or is already fighting, he may bite anyone who attempts to interfere. If you pick up a dog to protect it during a fight, he may bite you as he tries to get at the opposing dog, or the opposing dog may bite you in an effort to get at the dog you are holding. Their owners often lift small dogs up in order to protect them. In some cases, the attacking dog redirects its attention to the owner and lunges at him or her.

### Reasons for This Behavior

As a dog prepares to fight, his emotions affect his body chemistry and redirect its efforts from its normal requirements. Adrenaline is produced and secreted and circulates throughout his system, providing added energy and strength for the threatening physical ordeal. When dogs fight, their concentration is so sharply focused, it is almost impossible to communicate with them unless they are trained to perfection. The same is true of their emotional intensity. Interrupting a dogfight may cause a dog to redirect his aggression because he is no longer aware of whom he is biting.

# 2

# How Did He Get That Way?

The domestic dog is descended from the wolf and possesses many of the same behavior patterns. Although pet dogs living with humans are different in many ways, their response to various environmental factors or social interactions are remarkably similar to their wild, free-roaming cousins the wolves. This explains why some aggressive responses of a dog are normal while at the same time totally unacceptable to his family or to the community in which he lives.

When considering wolves or wild dogs and how they survive, common sense tells us that their aggressiveness is not only natural but necessary. As carnivores they must hunt down, capture, and take the life of the animals they eat. These are the expressions of aggressive behavior when hunger and survival are the motivation. The connection between predators and their prey animals leaves us no choice but to accept nature's disturbing harmony. The cruelty of the inevitable outcome of one animal stalking

another for food shows us an aspect of aggressive behavior with no apparent expressions of anger, only a desperate sprint for life between the hunter and the hunted. In contrast, a confrontation for dominance within a wolf pack is fought with snarling fury, although its ritualistic behavior lessens the danger to a great extent. Unlike the hunt, these confrontations do seem laced with anger but, paradoxically, rarely cause the loss of life. Aggressive behavior can also erupt over confrontations involving violations of pack discipline as well as encroachments of territory by non–pack members.

There is no behavioral inheritance more pronounced in the wolf as well as in some aggressive dogs than the defense of territory. The aggressive behavior of wolves is an important comparison with the behavior of aggressive dogs, especially if the dogs' behavior is threatening and dangerous to humans. Domestic-dog behavior is rooted in the natural behavior of wolves and dogs in the wild. Although we can only understand the *symptoms* of aggressiveness in dogs, not the causes, with absolute certainty, it is reasonable to think of them as outgrowths of their true inherent nature and, in many instances, distortions of it. The natural behavior of wolves, dogs, and other canids is inborn, characteristic of their species, and passed from one generation to the next. In that context, normal aggressive behavior is for the purpose of pack integrity, the hunt for food, and the protection of territory. To understand anything about the dogs we live with we must understand something about their nature.

## Natural Dog Behavior

In addition to the familiar qualities and unique personalities of individual dogs that you have probably known and loved, there are certain responses that can be considered natural dog behavior. Your dog's responses to events, circumstances, and sensory stimulation are somewhat predictable and have been developing over millions of years. These *general patterns* of behavior are inherited and have evolved into a biological reality for the family Canidae, which includes wolves, coyotes, jackals, hyenas, foxes, and wild and domestic dogs. They have been passed from generation to generation through the DNA (deoxyribonucleic acid) of each animal of each breed of each species. Dogs and their related species belong to the order Carnivora, or meat eaters. This fact has an important influence on the physical and behavioral characteristics that enable them to survive in nature and live compatibly with humans. Instinctive tactics, strategies, and other actions intended for survival, procreation, and protection have a direct bearing on the aggressive behavior of dogs as we know them.

All dogs have been genetically programmed to respond to specific stimulation in ways that are characteristic of their species. This is true of an eight-pound purebred ball of fluff living in the lap of luxury or an eighty-pound mixed breed roaming the city streets as part of a feral pack of dogs. Of course, living as domestic pets generation after generation with the imposed expectations of humans has modified dogs' natural behavior. Also, domesticity has removed the need for much of their natural aggressiveness. The families of pet dogs have assumed total responsibility for their food, shelter, and every conceivable aspect of survival. Domestication has produced a ripple or two in the evolutionary pool of canine behavior. Consequently, dangerous behavior in pet dogs has no natural function and can easily be interpreted as a distortion of what is accepted as normal for the average dog. Of course, this does not apply to the controlled aggressive behavior promoted by guard-dog training or the natural instinct to protect members of the family or perceived territory (see "Leader of the Pack" and "Territory," below).

Dogs have been living with humans for tens of thousands of years, and this has modified the behavior that would be necessary if they were living beyond the mortal coil of civilization. For example, a wolf that is the leader of his pack is an aggressive animal that asserts his dominance with frightening threats and at times harsh discipline. When dogs living with humans behave the same way, they are as abnormal as they are unacceptable.

Here then are the six essential elements of basic or instinctive canine behavior that forms the foundation on which the personality and qualities of domestic dogs rest.

It is important to note that after thousands of generations of domesticity, the behavior of some dogs has been modified from these basics, but only by degrees.

1. Wolves and dogs are pack animals and have an instinctive need to live in a group.
2. They form social attachments.
3. They require a leader for the survival of their pack.
4. They develop their own territory and vigorously protect it.
5. They sustain their lives by hunting for prey animals.
6. They mate, have puppies, and care for their young until they are self-sufficient.

## The Pack

The natural inclinations for wolves as well as dogs are to live as a group, hunt as a team, enforce pack structure, mate on a selective basis, and rear the young as a community. These are pack instincts, and they involve the need to live and work together. This is the society of dogs. When living as pets, dogs transfer this tendency to the human family as best they can. From the dog's point of view, living with people is another version of a pack, even if it consists of only one person and a dog. Because of the pack instinct, dogs thrive in our homes with the qualities we recognize and cherish, such as their uncommon friendship, their desire to please, their emotional attachment to us, and in many instances the protection they give. Most pet owners are certain that their dogs love them.

Every single skill that has been developed in specific dog breeds as a specialty is an everyday task for the members of a pack. Wolves or dogs living in a pack must help find prey animals by scent and by sight. The ability of specific dog breeds that were developed to herd (and protect) sheep and cattle, for example, springs from the inherent hunting skills of the wolf pack. Among their various tactics is the maneuver to scatter a herd of prey animals and chase them in the direction of other pack members who are waiting for them. In this way they separate the sick, the weak, or the very young so that they may capture them for food. All pack members will protect their kill from looters if necessary with the same ferocity with which some domestic dogs protect their territory. The aggressive behavior seen in domestic dogs is often an exaggeration, perhaps a distortion, of natural pack behavior with regard to chasing prey animals, establishing rank, or protecting territory.

Wolves are intolerant of outsiders that try to join an established pack. As a rule, the intruders are driven away as outcasts. These situations can provoke fights that can lead to bad endings for one or the other. This is especially the case when the food supply is low. This aspect of pack behavior has great significance for the domestic dog that continually chases or attacks other dogs or humans that enter his perceived territory. This fact helps us to understand the aggression of some dogs whose behavior seems unexplainable. The aggressive behavior of a domestic dog may be based on pure instinct rather than on some environmental factor. At times what seems illogical makes sense only when considering such a dog's relationship to his instincts. The life of the lone wolf is an existence that is imposed rather than chosen. A wolf on his own is limited in the hunt for food. He will be unable to capture a large prey animal without the help of other wolves and must settle for lesser game. A pack will survive where individuals cannot. A lone wolf leads a solitary existence that is incomplete and vulnerable to dangers that often lurk behind the next boulder.

A typical dog becomes part of a family, or pack, with unbelievable ease because of his social tendencies, his desire to live within a pack, and because of the human desire for his presence. Kind and loving treatment makes it work. Few mammals live in such highly organized groups as wolves, dogs, and humans. It is a natural arrangement.

## Social Attachments

Dogs create strong emotions in humans because of their need to live with others and because of their total acceptance of the care and love generously given to them. This behavior is an outgrowth of the instinct to maintain pack integrity and to behave as much as possible with gentleness and affection toward other members of the pack. The survival of the pack depends on its ability to establish territory, hunt effectively, procreate, and live in harmony. An important aspect of canid behavior involves the pairing of specific males with specific females for the purpose of mating and caring for their offspring.

The most durable form of social attachment is the *pair bond* created between a male and female wolf, which usually results in mating and the birth of cubs. Not every member of a wolf pack mates. The pack leader permits or prohibits individuals from being part of this process and very often excludes himself as well. Those in the pack who do not breed may become "aunts and uncles" and share the work needed to whelp and raise the cubs. Some males and females that have pair bonded go off together and form new packs. This is also true of some young wolves once they are able to survive on their own.

Inevitably, a strong, younger member of the pack will sooner or later challenge the leader for his position. Some social attachments within the pack may break when this happens. Old age and death have the same effect. These events have a temporary destabilizing effect. Once a new order of rank is established, the pack quickly accepts the new chain of command. Like wolves, domestic dogs also make meaningful social attachments, mostly with humans, but occasionally with other dogs (or other household pets). These are lasting relationships that in terms of human values are warm and loving friendships.

## Leader of the Pack

The survival of a wolf pack depends on leadership. A male wolf or dog becomes leader of the pack because of his assertive personality, aggressiveness, and in some instances his size and strength. A pack leader is one that asserts himself by sheer force of personality. The leader of the pack is referred to as the "Alpha wolf." The leadership is often shared with an Alpha female, who is subordinate to the Alpha male. This position is most often attained by force, which is aggressive behavior in its purest form. Wolves and dogs instinctively require a leader if their pack is to survive. This carries over to the family pet as well. Your dog will instinctively assume the role if no one else is perceived by him to be the leader. Dog owners should understand that a dog will accept leadership from those with dominant personalities or who behave with a degree of authority.

In the wild, dominant dogs or wolves eat first immediately after the hunt and have first choice of everything. The position of rank, which is usually established by aggressive behavior, is demonstrated early in a dog's life and can be seen in a litter of puppies at their mother's breast. There are always one or two that grab the most advantageous position for feeding and one or two that must struggle for any position at all. Rank is also apparent in play-fighting. A litter of puppies can be viewed as a microcosm of an adult pack. At times the aggressive play of puppies transforms into flashes of serious conflicts that end as quickly as they begin. If the young dogs remain together as a group beyond sixteen weeks, their personalities become set as dominant or subordinate dogs.

A very serious-looking leader that is feared and obeyed dominates every wolf pack or dog pack. The entire pack looks to him for his reaction to anything out of the ordinary before responding, such as an intruder entering the inner core of their territory. The leader of the pack controls the hunt, fights challengers, and demands submission from the pack on all issues.

The leader's assertion of dominance is seen when he stands straight with his ears erect and his tail held in a stiff, motionless position. He will stare at his adversary with intense and unblinking eyes. His large teeth may become exposed behind curling lips as he sends out a menacing growl from his throat. This is enough to frighten most challengers and usually resolves all questions as the subordinate wolf assumes a lower posture and flattens his ears as he tucks his tail between his legs. If an actual fight ensues, dominance is established when the leader stands over his challenger, who is on his back exposing his underbelly and throat in a gesture of submission. It is a gesture that can be seen in puppies when they lie on their back with their paws bent forward. This ritualized behavior ends the fight, resolves the question, and all things return to normal.

In the winter, the wolves keep a steady pace as they move through the wind and snow in a single line, each stepping into the tracks made by the one in front of him. At the head of the line is the Alpha. He finds the trail, parts the snowdrifts with his body, establishes tracks for the others to step in, and guides them to better hunting. He is the leader of the pack.

## Territory

The territory of wolves can be as small as ten to fifteen square miles or as large as hundreds of square miles. The social organization of the wolf is based on the pack, which cannot be sustained without a territory. The size of the pack almost never exceeds what the food in the territory can provide. Without a territory, wolves will not mate or produce new litters of cubs. Territory is acquired by a pack after it has been vacated by others or is developed in a new area.

A territory usually has many paths and trails in it, which are used by other animals and other wolf packs for passage. Members of a pack do not usually fight to defend every square mile within their hunting range. However, they become seriously aggressive about intrusions into the inner core of their territory, which is an area used for sleeping, eating, and performing various life functions.

Because wolves are somewhat nomadic in their constant search for food, the inner core changes as they move about their large hunting range. The inner core involves a den, which may be a cave, a tunnel, or hollowed-out logs, and is important for whelping. In our homes a dog may regard the crate he sleeps in as the inner core of his territory, or a corner of the room, the whole room, or the entire house with its surrounding property. Some dogs consider their neighborhood their territory, or the entire city they live in, and become agitated or dangerous when anyone enters it. This is an example of territorial/overprotective aggression.

## Hunting

Finding, stalking, and chasing after prey animals are important aspects of the hunt for food. The wolves' highly developed senses of smell, sight, and hearing allow them to perform this part of the process with great skill. Another aspect of finding prey is remembering the trails the migrating herds use to cross their range. Hunting skills also involve inventive strategies and tactics for chasing a herd into the waiting jaws of the pack; separating animals from their herd so they can be captured; and the pack's techniques for attacking large animals despite their size. Many of these hunting behaviors are inherently part of the dog's nature. They are always close to the surface, waiting to react to those things that set them in motion. Ironically, dogs that live as pets have no need to hunt, considering how well fed they are by their families, but may still exhibit hunting behaviors once they are triggered.

Dogs that are bred to herd sheep and cattle have been developed and trained for only a few of their natural hunting skills. The same is true of dogs that are bred for guard work. Terriers are specialized hunters that will "go to ground" after a fox or other tunneling animal, such as a rabbit, gopher, mouse, and so on. Bird dogs locate their quarry, indicate where they are, and retrieve them once they have been shot. The various hound breeds were developed by breeders to find and stalk their prey with the use of their well-developed sense of smell or sight. Greyhounds, Whippets, Afghans, Salukis, and other coursing hounds not only sight their prey but are also swift enough to outrun it.

Chasing anything or anyone that runs from a dog is a basic hunting instinct. He does not have to be hungry, angry, or threatened to chase an animal or a person that moves quickly past his line of sight. Giving chase is an instinctive hunting response. It does not take much to trigger it in many dogs, especially if they are aggressive.

## Mating

The process of reproduction and raising a litter produces aggressive behavior in adult dogs as well as in wolves. For example, males often must fight other males for the privilege of mating. A lactating female becomes aggressive if an unwelcome creature gets too close to her puppies or endangers them in any perceived way. A male wolf never enters the den of a lactating female for the first two or three weeks of the new litter's birth or he will suffer her wrath. He simply deposits food for her outside the den and leaves quickly.

The differences between dogs and wolves, however, are most clearly seen in their sexual and reproductive behavior. Typically, female dogs go in heat (estrus) twice a year.

Female wolves go in heat only once a year. This is an important difference when it comes to acceptance of the male by a female. Females not in heat become aggressive with sexually assertive males and fearlessly reject their overtures. Female wolves mate once a year, while female dogs mate twice a year (if allowed or circumstances permit). This difference between the two species is probably due in part to the limitation on population that nature seems to have imposed on the wolf pack. Its survival is based on the size of its hunting range and the food it can yield. A pack with too many mouths to feed could easily exhaust the availability of food. Nature seems to have provided the solution with fewer estrous cycles and greater competition for mating, resulting in a limited wolf population. This is not the case for domestic dogs.

Male dogs express their sexuality differently from females. They are much more aggressive about sex and will mate with any receptive female. They tend to roam greater distances from home and require more effort to obedience-train. When close to a female in heat, even the best-trained dog becomes unreliable, unmanageable, and aggressive if thwarted from his pursuit. During the time of estrus, the owner of a female must prevent his or her dog from getting loose and mating with a nearby male. Besides causing unwanted pregnancies, such encounters can also cause injuries from aggressive behavior.

## How Aggressive Behavior Is Created

Natural dog behavior as described above is the genetic foundation on which canine aggression rests. However, aggressiveness can also be the result of specific experiences. A variety of external influences can provoke aggressive behavior temporarily or as a permanent, generalized form of responses and reactions. Some dogs are born aggressive, while others have aggressiveness thrust upon them. This is important information for those people who are looking for a new puppy as well as for those who already have a dog with aggressive tendencies. If you understand the conditions that create the problem, it is possible to avoid it, alter it to some degree, learn to manage it in a reasonable way, or at least understand the dangers involved and do what is necessary. In many cases it is not too late to save the situation. *The most disastrous aspect of canine aggression, however, is human denial.* Here then is a brief catalog of many of the causes of canine aggression.

## Inherited Behavior – the Genetic Factor

Scientific evidence points in the direction of inherited behavior as an important cause of canine aggression. If either of the parents of a litter of puppies is an aggressive or shy dog, it is very likely that some or all of their puppies are going to inherit that behavior. This has proven to be the experience of so many breeders and dog professionals that the concept is widely accepted. Researchers have established reliable evidence that many behaviors, including aggressiveness, are inherited. Genetic behavior is a relatively new scientific discipline, with important research supporting the concept. Most current thinking on this subject is based on the published research papers of John Paul Scott in his groundbreaking books *Animal Behavior* and *Dog Behavior: The Genetic Basis,* with John L. Fuller (University of Chicago Press, 1988). Experience has taught us that dogs that have inherited their aggressive behavior can be identified in the first six or seven weeks of their lives.

Breeding good dogs involves science, intelligence, skill, and integrity. The best breeders have demonstrated time and time again that they can produce puppies of choice by selecting the parents according to type, size, coat, or temperament. To skillfully produce a litter of healthy, even-tempered puppies with a particular look requires a good bit of learning and experience. You must possess knowledge of genetics and genetic codes, have information about and experience with the breed of choice, have the ability to understand and interpret a pedigree, and know how to scrutinize the selected dogs for possible faults — all this in addition to knowing how to mate dogs properly. The best breeders select dogs for their good health, even temperament, and conformation standards. When dogs are bred indiscriminately for profit or in ignorance of inherited characteristics, the possibility is increased substantially for producing unhealthy, aggressive, or shy dogs that may not even resemble their breed. The genetic factor is the wild card of canine aggression and must not be ignored.

## The Source of the Dog

In light of genetics and its impact on aggressive behavior, you must consider the source of your dog an important factor in aggressive behavior. If he comes from a reputable breeder with years of experience and who has an investment in producing quality animals, your chances of acquiring a good dog are much better than from most other sources. This is a much more acceptable way to find the right dog than from an individual who placed an ad in a newspaper or from a pet store. In either of those situations you will probably be buying a dog without having any knowledge of its mother or father and with no family history or pedigree.

Some misguided people want dogs that are aggressive and go looking for that trait from amateur breeders without realizing what they are getting into. If the breeder is simply someone who bred his dog over the back fence with no thought about temperament, personality, or medical history, your chances of acquiring a problematic dog is quite high. It is equally risky buying a dog in a pet store. Most pet shops get their puppies ("livestock") from the so-called puppy mills, which are usually found in rural areas. A puppy mill can be an addition to a small farm or it can be a large operation run like a factory. It is almost always a facility that maintains cramped, dirty kennels jammed with dogs forced to live in horrendous, inhumane conditions. Adult males and females are constantly mating and giving birth to puppies in large quantities.

At a puppy mill mating does not take into consideration the medical history of the dogs or of their parents or grandparents, or their good or bad physical and mental qualities. Every dog that breathes is mated, as if on an assembly line. Unhealthy dogs born from unhealthy parents are not excused from the obligation to mate. The goal is to produce as many puppies as possible with as little expenditure as necessary. No doubt some good dogs come from some pet shops, but there is no way for inexperienced dog owners to know what they are getting. Dogs from pet shops are usually purebred animals with registration papers to prove it. However, these papers have no bearing on the quality or lack of quality of the dog, especially with regard to temperament or inherited medical problems.

Dogs from puppy mills are usually transported by truck and then by air and then by truck again in flimsy shipping containers stacked in cold or hot baggage holds. They have not been socialized or introduced to human handling or kindness at any stage of their young lives. Those that survive the trip are probably traumatized from it. Once they arrive at the pet shop, they may be dropped into a pet store window display with dozens of strange dogs from different litters. If one animal gets sick, they all get sick, or carry the disease to other dogs. These many needful puppies begin on their own to behave as dominant or subordinate dogs. If a buyer is lucky enough to get a healthy pup under these conditions, the dog may very well have developed behavior problems that do not seem to be serious until months later. Pet shop dogs are riskier than dogs from noncommercial breeders. The unfortunate fact is, however, that many, many dogs are purchased from pet shops. If the store operator tells you he gets his dogs from reputable, local breeders, it is probably untrue, because no reputable breeder would sell his or her puppies to a pet shop.

The sources for getting a dog are breeders, pet shops, veterinarians, notices in supermarkets, newspaper ads, neighbors, and, of course, animal rescue shelters. No matter where you go for a dog or puppy, give him a personality test and evaluation, as described in chapter 3, "How Aggressive *Is* Your Dog? Tests and Signs of Aggression." This will give you an opportunity to avoid getting one that is aggressive.

## Socialization

A major cause of aggressiveness in dogs is the failure to socialize puppies in the early part of their lives. The lack of early socialization creates dogs that are fearful, distrustful, or antagonistic toward humans and other dogs. Dogs that are not socialized have little or no adaptability to unfamiliar people or new situations. They are also difficult to obedience-train or control. Most significantly, unsocialized dogs are almost always aggressive and can become dangerous.

The socializing of dogs has two aspects to it. The first has to do with a specific technique applied to puppies during the first few weeks of their lives that influences their behavioral development in positive ways. All experienced, caring dog breeders know about the critical period in the life of every puppy that, according to the studies of Scott and Fuller, begins on the twenty-first day of life and continues to the forty-ninth day. During this critical period

breeders apply the simple technique of gently and lovingly holding the young pups at least once a day. As a result, the puppies have a much greater chance of realizing their full potential as adaptive pet dogs with a willingness to be trained by humans and live in their homes. Socialized dogs are also adaptive to other pets and friendly dogs.

The second aspect of socialization has to do with the way a puppy is raised and allowed to live as he grows into adulthood. When he is fed properly, touched frequently, played with, spoken to in loving and friendly terms, and encouraged to bond with those in his family, with no effort at all he becomes a socialized dog. A dog that lives inside a warm, friendly home, with a loving family, experiencing the sounds and noises of everyday life, relating to new people coming and going, is bound to be a happy, friendly pet — in other words, *socialized*.

By contrast, puppies tend to grow into shy, fearful, aggressive dogs when raised in the opposite manner. This is the case if they are taken away from their mothers and littermates too soon, get little or no nurturing from humans, are raised in the backyard, or are left most of the time in isolation or near isolation. Dogs raised in near isolation cannot adjust to the ordinary sounds of life around them and react with aggression to anyone or anything that comes too close. Dogs who do not interact in a friendly way with a variety of people on a daily basis and are raised in this unsocialized manner are living in a way that is unnatural for their species. They will fear or distrust almost everyone who comes close or who enters their territory, with the exception of those who feed them. Such dogs become aggressive very early in life.

Some dogs become aggressive because they are socialized or bonded to one or more dogs in the house rather than to the humans in the family. The dog that is raised with another dog as a puppy will not necessarily be socialized with people, even if the dog is loved. A socialized puppy that is to adapt to people must be shown affection and given individual attention by the family to avoid too much influence from another dog in the house. An adult dog that is social only with other dogs can become aggressive toward or fearful of humans.

## Misguided Owner Behavior

Abusive treatment, bad handling, or errors in judgment are the most common causes of aggressive behavior in dogs. Human influences can often modify the behavior of normal dogs and make them aggressive. Eventually, such dogs become totally unacceptable in the human environment.

Among the most aggressive behaviors are growling, nipping, lunging, biting, chasing, refusing to obey commands, ignoring owners, blocking one's path, barking at individuals in an extremely threatening manner, and mounting. Most dogs do not bite unless they have been provoked, encouraged, or frightened. If a dog is physically punished or hit for any reason, he is going to either defend himself aggressively or cower, or both. The only defense a dog has is his ability to bite, since he does not have hands with which to hit back. As with children, hitting a dog is the same as teaching him to be violent. Fighting fire with fire only causes more fire. A common misconception about dealing with problem behavior is to punish a dog by hitting, hollering, threatening, pointing accusing fingers, or rubbing his nose in his housebreaking mistakes. This is an effort that guarantees the creation of a fearful, aggressive dog. Puppies are full of energy and mischief. It is normal for them to get into trouble, just like human toddlers trying out their legs for the first time. If you hit or cuff or slap a puppy, he is going to fear you. If your hands are used for affection, your puppy will never flinch when you go near him. If your hands are associated with pain or rejection, then he is going to avoid anything that has to do with your hands. To hit a dog of any age is to abuse him and start him on the road to aggressive behavior.

One of the greatest mistakes dog owners make is trying to turn their pets into protection dogs. Few understand that this can only be accomplished with techniques used by experts who specialize in the field of protection training. A trained protection dog is a skilled working animal that is always under control and obeys commands instantly and precisely. He will react aggressively only on command or if his handler is apparently being threatened. Not all dogs are suited for this purpose. The trained protection dog is like a loaded weapon that must be handled with skill, control, good judgment, and knowledge of the legal responsibilities involved. Protection-training by amateurs is potentially harmful to everyone who comes in contact with their dogs, including the owners themselves. The methods amateurs use usually include isolating the dog, never allowing him to be friendly to anyone, and rewarding him for barking or biting. These are, without a doubt, the very worst ways to raise a dog, especially a protection dog. All they accomplish is to create an unfriendly, frightening, antisocial dog that is uncontrollable and indiscriminate about whom he chases, attacks, or bites.

These are the proverbial "junkyard dogs" that are so dangerous.

Another misguided human behavior that creates aggression in dogs is the failure to provide leadership and authority, along with the failure to control the dog. All dogs require a leader. If you are not the dog's leader, he will become your leader, and this will result in aggressive behavior toward you and other humans. A dog that is born with a dominant personality must not be allowed to take over a household and do whatever he wants. All dogs must be under the control of the humans with whom they live, especially those with dominant personalities. A dominant dog is not a vicious dog. He simply wants to be top dog. If he behaves badly, he must be corrected and not allowed to get away with it. An adult dominant dog can be quite frightening because he may look happy as he wags his tail, while at the same time he stares you down, daring you to make a move. You always know where you stand with a fear-aggressive dog because he barks, growls, and backs away and can bite when you turn around to leave. This is especially true if he is cornered.

Of major importance is understanding that your dog's behavior will reflect how he lives and how he is handled, and how he is treated. Aggressiveness that has been inherited is the exception. If you start out with a normal puppy, it is possible to avoid the creation of aggressive behavior based on the information provided in this chapter. If it already exists in your dog, it can be changed or brought under control with proper handling, obedience-training, and the application of the correct training techniques for the special problems caused by its behavior. If you create a more pleasant environment, you will have a more pleasant dog. If you have made mistakes, it is not too late to correct them. If you have been yelling at your dog, it is time to stop. If you have been hitting your dog, by all means stop. No matter how many dogs you may have had, you are not expected to know what a professional dog trainer knows. It is time to learn to communicate properly with your dog and throw out useless concepts of the past and start out with a fresh slate. We advise you to use the next two chapters of this book to first, obedience-train your aggressive dog, and second, solve his specific aggressive-behavior problems — in that order. This may be the most important thing you have ever done for your dog and for yourself. Good luck.

# 3

# How Aggressive *Is* Your Dog?
*Tests and Signs of Aggression*

The purpose of this chapter is to help you determine if your dog is aggressive and into which category of aggression he fits. Many people have a hard time accepting the reality of their dog's aggressive behavior. For a variety of reasons they drift in and out of denial as if in a dream world where everything magically works itself out. The consequences of the family dog's aggressive behavior rudely awaken such dreamers, but by then it is usually too late. If someone gets bitten, there is a price to pay. Such persons love their dogs very much and may make every excuse imaginable for their pet's unacceptable and dangerous behavior, just like the parents of troubled kids. When their dogs behave aggressively, they try to justify it for fear of losing the dog's love, for fear of losing the dog, or for fear of making difficult but necessary changes. Rationalizations such as "He's just being protective," or "He's

just being playful," or "He's never done that before" are often heard. Be that as it may, if a dog growls, bares his teeth, or bites, it is impossible to avoid the unpleasant truth that he is aggressive and potentially dangerous.

You can get an accurate evaluation of your dog's aggressiveness with the simple tests and observations offered in this chapter. An evaluation of your dog's aggressiveness is essential if you want to change his behavior. For example, aggression from a fearful dog must be dealt with differently than aggression from a dog that is too dominant. The following six tests and nine areas in which to observe your dog are easy to carry out. The interpretation of their results requires nothing more than common sense. Despite the simplicity of these procedures, they have proven to be highly effective and helpful to thousands of dogs and their anguished families. These are tried-and-true procedures. In many cases this is the last best chance you may have to save your situation.

## Testing for Aggression

These tests have been effectively used by the National Institute of Dog Training for three decades and have helped evaluate more than thirty-five thousand dogs. With an evaluation based on the tests in this chapter, you should be able to determine your dog's category of aggression and initiate appropriate methods of training and reconditioning. By carefully considering the section "The Dog's Response and What It Means" after each test, you will understand the results of each test. The ability to recognize the various forms of canine aggression will give you important insights into your dog's unwanted behavior.

All of these tests can be given in your own home if you already own a dog. Several of them are especially useful for selecting a puppy. These are the Dominant Stare Test, the Physical-Sensitivity Test, and the Rollover Test. They could help you avoid making a major mistake in your selection of a pet. When giving the following tests you must always have a leash and training collar on the dog to retain control of him for safety reasons. No matter how well you may think you know your dog, administering these tests may bring out aggressive behaviors never exhibited in front of you before. Obviously, the size of your dog, his level of aggressive behavior, and the nature of his behavior should determine the intensity with which you conduct these tests. A dog that snarls, curls his lip, or attempts to bite requires a greater amount of caution than one that does not.

## Caution Levels

If your dog is:

***Seven weeks to six months***: All tests can be given with little risk.

***Six months to one year***: Use caution when giving tests.

***One year to three years (or older)***: Use extreme caution when giving tests.

## The Dominant Stare Test

This test will determine if your dog was born dominant or subordinate. A dominant dog is frequently called a Top dog, Alpha dog, or leader of the pack. A dog that would be leader of the pack may also want to be leader of his human family and is going to be aggressive. In such cases it is important to determine whether or not your dog is dominant

so you can prepare for his potentially aggressive behavior while he is still young or cope with it if he is an adult.

**The Test.** Administer this test in both indoor and outdoor environments. Have one person hold the leash for safety reasons, while another administers the test.

Stand approximately ten feet away and call your dog's name to get his attention. He should be looking straight at you, making direct eye contact. Stare into his eyes. Using body language, assume an authoritative posture. Lean forward. Use no verbal communication at this time. Repeat this test once in the home and again in the backyard. Both of these areas are a dog's territories.

To obtain the most accurate results, you may want to administer this test using both family members and people not familiar with the dog.

**The Dog's Response and What It Means.** *If your dog is dominant,* he will look directly into your eyes and not break the stare or look away. He may even curl his lip or growl. His tail and ears may become erect and point straight up. His body will appear to grow larger. He may freeze in his position or slowly move toward you. If he does not break his stare and maintains direct eye contact with you, he is sending you the message that he's dominant over you. If this happens, you should break off eye contact and look away immediately so that you don't antagonize him or accelerate his aggression. A dominant dog automatically takes charge of the family and the house. Situations that threaten his leadership position or the command of his territory will lead to serious aggression. (See "Dominant Aggression" in chapter 1.)

**Dominant Dog**

**Submissive Dog**

*If your dog is subordinate,* he will break eye contact and look away, submitting to your dominance over him. A subordinate dog knows that you (the administrator of the test) are the leader of the pack and in charge of protecting the family's territory and well-being. Some dogs may be subordinate only with you and behave in a dominant manner with all others, including the rest of your family.

## The Food Test

This test will determine if your dog is food-aggressive. Such behavior may be caused by territorial aggression, dominant aggression, or an exaggerated survival instinct, or it may have been acquired from past experiences as a stray dog. A previous owner who encouraged the behavior could have created these unacceptable responses. Food-aggressive behavior can start in the first seven weeks of a dog's life as the result of fighting littermates for food. It is important to determine if your dog is food-aggressive, because feeding your dog is a daily occurrence, and you (or a child) are likely to get bitten if you touch your dog's food bowl. This may happen even if you just get near the bowl. Getting bitten is almost a certainty if you try to take his bowl away with or without food in it. Ironically, this may happen even if you are trying to add food to the bowl. The results of this test will provide you with important knowledge about your dog with regard to your safety.

**The Test.** There are three ways of testing for food aggression:

1. Place your dog in a wire crate if you have one (see the Solutions Key in chapter 5, "Solving Your

Dog's Aggressive-Behavior Problems") and feed him while he is in it with the wire door closed. Approach him as he eats and observe his behavior.

2. If you do not have a crate, a common plastic child gate or puppy gate can be used instead. Place it in a doorway separating one room from another. Put the food near the gate. Approach the dog from the opposite side as he eats and observe his behavior.

3. **(Exercise caution when using the following method of testing.)** Put a leash and collar on the dog. Fill the dog's food bowl with his favorite meal and place it in his regular feeding area. Stand six feet away, at the end of the leash, as he begins eating. Have someone walk into the room while the dog continues to eat. Be sure you are holding the leash securely. If there is no aggressive behavior at this point, have the person slowly walk toward the dog, observing his behavior. If he starts to growl, the person should immediately stop approaching him.

**The Dog's Response and What It Means.** If the dog growls, curls his lip, or snaps at you, he is food-aggressive (see, "Possessive Aggression" in chapter 1). If the dog does not respond aggressively, it means he is not food aggressive. This test is not limited to food. There are other objects, such as toys, rawhide chews, and so on, over which a dog might become aggressive. Administer the same test to check for an aggressive reaction to other possessions.

## The Punishment-Reaction Test

This is a test that will determine if a dog has been hit or threatened on any part of the body, or pointed at and verbally disciplined, or dominated in any other negative manner. A fearful or aggressive reaction to this test indicates behavior that has been acquired, usually from being verbally or physically punished. It is important to determine your dog's reaction to this test because so much communication with him involves the use of your hands. A punishment-aggressive dog may bite if you wave your hands in front of him.

**The Test.** This test should be administered with the dog by your side, under control with the leash and collar on. Someone not living with the dog should give this test. Standing approximately six feet in front of the dog, he or she should simulate making a striking motion as if about to hit him with a hand or a rolled-up newspaper, then point a finger at the dog and say, "What did you do?" *DO NOT HIT THE DOG. THIS IS MERELY A TEST.*

**The Dog's Response and What It Means.** If the dog has been hit in the past, he may react in one of two ways:

1. He may snarl, growl, lunge, or even bite.
2. He may flinch or duck his head in a cowering fashion. He may try to run away. If cornered, he may bark, growl, or bite.

If your dog has never been hit or verbally abused, he will have none of the above reactions and will look unconcerned. If he reacts with fear or aggression, he has been either hit or disciplined in a negative manner in the past and may bite if he feels at risk from hand movements that appear to be threatening.

## The Physical-Sensitivity Test

The purpose of this test is to determine if your dog has an unusually low tolerance for minor pain and discomfort. A physically sensitive dog will behave aggressively with anyone who causes even the most minor irritation of his body. Unfortunately, young children are the most likely to get bitten because they often pull at the dog's body during play. A snap or bite may also stem from dogs suffering from a painful medical condition, such as hip dysplasia. The minor aches and pains of old age or arthritis will provoke an aggressive response to being touched on a sensitive part of the body. Improper grooming techniques will also produce a surprising reaction to the most minor pinch or pull. *It is important to understand that many physically sensitive dogs have inherited their intolerance for minor pain and respond aggressively to even the most trivial irritations.*

**The Test.** Use a quiet area for this procedure with no one else present. You must control your dog with a leash and collar to avoid getting bitten. If your dog is physically sensitive, he may snap or bite during this test. Use the fingers of one hand to test the dog while holding him by the leash with the other.

The first part of this test involves pulling the dog's skin with your left hand as you restrain him with the leash in your right hand. Start pulling the skin at his shoulders, gently at first and then gradually increasing the intensity.

Pull at his skin at the middle part of his body in the same manner, gently, then with greater pressure. Continue by pulling the dog's skin at his rump in the same way.

The final portion of this test involves the tail. Hold the dog in place with the leash and collar. Grab the tail and pull it gently at first, then stretching it out with greater force.

**The Dog's Response and What It Means.** The dog may react in one of the following ways to having his skin pulled:

1. He may growl and attempt to snap or bite without warning.
2. He may scream, try to bite your hand and run away, or cower as if being hurt.
3. He may become oversubmissive or dominant, depending on his personality.

4. He may simply look at you as if it were a game, showing no signs of aggression.

The dog may react in one of the following ways to having his tail pulled:

1. He may bite and growl no matter how slight the pull.
2. He may barely tolerate this and may howl or scream.
3. He may curl his lips, snap at you, and try to get away.
4. He may turn around and look at you with curiosity, seemingly unbothered, and may even become playful.

The dog's reactions are easy to interpret. If he reacts aggressively or in any extreme manner to being pulled at, he is obviously physically sensitive. The degree to which he is sensitive to minor irritation is determined by the intensity of his reaction. Some dogs may be sensitive on the rump only, while others show it on the tail or some other part of the body. The dog's reactions to these tests should indicate to you how to handle him and how to avoid giving him pain and the aggressive behavior it causes.

## The Rollover Test

The purpose of this test is to determine if your dog has inherited dominant or subordinate tendencies. With this information you can begin to relate to him in a safe, non-threatening, yet effective, manner. Being able to identify your dog's inherited behavioral tendencies will help you manage him in ways that are appropriate for him and the world he inhabits. The usefulness of this knowledge will be apparent when you obedience-train or attempt to solve your dog's behavior problems.

If you roll your dog over and he just lies there or he wriggles around playfully, he is probably not aggressive. If he growls, snarls, snaps, or bites, you can be sure that he is aggressive. An aggressive dog will struggle to get up, curl his lips, and behave in a variety of aggressive ways. In the Rollover Test, your dog's responses will not only establish whether he is aggressive or not, but also help you determine the type of aggression with which you must cope. Some dogs will react with fear as you place them on their back. They'll cry and scream and struggle to get free even though you're not hurting them. Other dogs may react by staring daggers at you, growling, and possibly attacking you in a dominant manner. Obviously, a dog that is fearful or dominant is going to be more dangerous than one that isn't. The Rollover Test will reveal these specific aggressive inclinations.

**The Test.** *Caution: If you are unsure about your dog's aggressiveness, use a soft nylon muzzle when applying this procedure to avoid getting bitten. (See "Training Equipment" in chapter 4, "How to Obedience-Train an Aggressive Dog.")*

Administer this test in a quiet area indoors or outdoors with no one else present. Place a leash and collar on the dog and use them to maintain firm control. Quickly but gently roll your dog onto his back before he has a chance to think about it. Do not place him on his side. He must be rolled directly onto his back with his spine lying flat against the ground. Bend over the dog, with both legs

straddling his body. If this is not possible, kneel beside him. When you lean over the dog, you place him in a position that makes him feel completely vulnerable. Hold the leash with your left hand and gently but firmly grasp the dog's skin with your right hand, just beneath the dog's collar. Remain neutral and do not respond to your dog's reactions to the test. Do not hold the dog's skin for more than fifteen to thirty seconds.

A truly dominant dog may not allow this test to be performed. In the process of rolling him over onto his back, you may hear the warning sign of growling. If this happens, discontinue the test; you'll already know he has aggressive tendencies.

**The Dog's Response and What It Means.** The dog may react in any of the following ways:

1. He may growl and curl his lips.
2. He may try to bite you.
3. He may make direct eye contact and stare hard at you.
4. He may struggle to get away.
5. He may scream, yelp, or whine loudly.
6. He may place his body in a submissive position.
7. He may wet.
8. He may behave in a fearful, shy manner but also try to bite you.
9. He may be relaxed or playful.

A dominant-aggressive dog might respond with deep growls, lip curling, or by trying to bite you. He might make direct eye contact with you in an attempt to get out of the subordinate position.

A fear-aggressive dog may growl or try to get away, depending on the intensity of his fear. He may cry or scream, as if in pain. However, that response is an expression of emotion rather than an outcry of physical pain. His body will probably be in a submissive position, with his front and back legs folding together. He will show all the behavior of a shy dog but in addition may try to bite you.

A dog that is not dominant-aggressive or fear-aggressive will be relaxed or playful.

After completing these six tests, you will know whether or not you live with a dominant-aggressive or fear-aggressive dog. This helps you understand a great deal more about your dog's actions, reactions, and personality than ever before. With this information you can more readily communicate with your aggressive dog and train him effectively.

### Signs of Aggression

Although the tests in the first part of this chapter help you to evaluate your dog, there is also much to be learned by simply looking at his day-to-day behavior. Unfortunately, many dog owners do not recognize the less obvious signs of canine aggression. Their dog's eccentric behavior is all too often accepted as normal. If a dog bites into his bowl, spills the water all over the floor, and then tosses the bowl against the kitchen wall like a tennis ball, he is more likely to get a laugh than the correction he needs. The dog's family may not *get it* even if he growls when they try to take the bowl out of his mouth. Nevertheless, when a dog refuses to let go of the bowl and growls when you touch it, watch out. This is an important sign of aggressive behavior that must be understood as a warning from the dog. He is saying that he will bite you if you persist.

As you observe your dog for aggressiveness, common sense makes it all so clear. Looking for the signs of aggression is a new way of thinking about your dog. Open your eyes and you will gain new insights. Simply observing your dog will enable you to see the signs of aggression and then use some of the reconditioning solutions offered in chapters 4 and 5. Even if you cannot solve an aggression problem, you can learn how to control it. Controlling your dog may be the one factor that decides his fate.

*If your dog has not bitten anyone up to this point, consider yourself lucky, but this could change at any time. The following*

signs of aggression are the warning signals you must take seriously to avoid having your dog hurt someone. If your dog growls
at you or anyone else at any time, any place, or for any reason,
it is a problem with dangerous consequences. If your dog snarls,
curls his lips, tries to mount people, lunges, snaps, blocks your
path, or barks aggressively, his next action could be to bite.
These are behaviors that can appear in any aggressive dog,
whether he is shy or dominant. Some dog owners believe that
their dogs do not bite because they haven't caused the need for
stitches or haven't broken the skin after a snapping incident.
This is a risky attitude because such dogs can become dangerous at any time. These signs of aggression practically guarantee
a biting incident at some point. Here then is a list of the areas
and events where the signs of canine aggression can be seen. If
your dog shows aggressive behavior in connection with any of
the following situations, his behavior problems must be addressed.

## Signs of Aggression: In the Kitchen or Dining Room

When the dog is eating and someone walks by his food
bowl

When the dog steals food and someone tries to take it
away from him

When the dog is under the table during a meal and
someone (especially a child) drops food on the floor and
reaches for it

When someone tries to stop the dog as he digs into a
garbage can

When two dogs of the same sex are being fed at the same
time

**How Aggressive *Is* Your Dog?**

## Signs of Aggression: In the Bedroom

When the dog is on his owner's bed and someone tries to remove him

Whenever or wherever the dog is moved or touched

When someone enters the room, whether it is a member of the family or a perfect stranger

When the dog is allowed to sleep on the bed and is moved off by his owner's spouse or companion, especially if he is accidentally awakened

When the dog is under the bed and someone tries to reach for him, causing him to feel trapped or unusually territorial

## Signs of Aggression: In the Family Room

When the dog is being removed from the furniture

When the dog cannot understand the difference between his possessions and those belonging to a child

## Signs of Aggression: At the Front Door

When a delivery person or other stranger enters the front door

When the dog barks and then backs away, stays at the owner's side, and then chases a stranger when he or she leaves

When the dog is startled by a sudden movement

**GRRR!**

When someone reaches out to give the owner something or to shake hands

### Signs of Aggression: In a Child's Room

When visiting children play with the dog as if he were their own

During roughhousing

When children tease or pull on parts of the dog's body

When a child falls on top of the dog

When the dog steals a child's toy and the child tries to take it back

When an adult is holding the dog, and a child approaches

When the dog is not familiar with small children and is suddenly exposed to a newborn baby or a visiting child

### Signs of Aggression: In the Front and Backyard

When the dog is loose during a delivery

When the dog is tied up and someone enters his area

When the dog is growling at the fence as people go by

When strangers approach the dog and reach down to pet him or corner him

## Signs of Aggression: In Public

When the dog is on a leash and lunges at joggers, bikers, or rollerbladers who go by

When another dog passes

When a stranger approaches the owner, acts friendly, and reaches for the dog to pet him

When the dog is tied up in a park

When a small dog is being held by his owner, and someone approaches

When the dog chases anything that moves

When the dog is handled by a professional service provider, such as a veterinarian or a groomer

When certain parts of the dog's body are touched during an examination

When someone is standing over the dog, making him feel dominated or fearful

When the dog is in a veterinarian's waiting room, and another person or another dog comes too close

## Signs of Aggression: In a Car

When a stranger approaches the car

When the dog sees another dog and the owner uses his hands to quiet the dog or move him out of the way

When the dog is moved off the seat that is his perceived territory

## Signs of Aggression: Other Areas to Observe

When the dog is blocking a doorway

When the dog is being verbally or physically corrected

When the dog sees new people

When medication is given to the dog

When you put his collar on the dog

When the dog growls at any member of the family

When you try to pick up the dog and move him off the furniture

When the dog is sleeping and he is startled when you wake him

When you approach the dog in "his territory"

By now you should understand how useful it is to test your dog for aggressive behavior as well as to be able to recognize the signs of his aggression. It is impossible to improve your situation until you understand it. Now that you have assessed your dog, you need to move to the next important step, which is to begin the process of changing his behavior. Chapters 5, 6, and 7 address this issue in very specific ways. However, more aggressive-behavior problems in pet dogs are solved as a result of obedience-training than from any other approach. The most important step you can take begins in chapter 4, "How to Obedience-Train an Aggressive Dog."

# 4

# How to Obedience-Train an Aggressive Dog

It is possible to make an aggressive dog less threatening and more pleasant to live with if he is obedience-trained. Changing your aggressive dog's behavior begins with obedience training, which is a conditioning process that will modify his behavior and give you control over him. *You cannot begin to solve any aggressive-behavior problems if your dog is not trained.* An aggressive dog, however, requires techniques that are modifications of those normally used in a basic obedience course.

You must first consider your dog's level of aggression. Is he a biter, a growler, or just a barking bully? How to adjust the training should be based on the form your dog's aggression takes, which can be determined from the first three chapters of this book, including the tests described in chapter 3. Is your dog *fear*-aggressive, *dominant*-aggressive, *territorial*-aggressive, *possessive*-aggressive, or a combina-

tion of any of the ten categories described in chapter 1? Weighing these factors will help you train him according to your own common sense and the dictates of his behavior. For example, you would handle a dog that growls at you differently than one that doesn't. If your dog growls, he is threatening to bite you if you continue doing whatever it is that you are doing. In that situation, or if he becomes menacing during a training session, we advise you to place a soft nylon muzzle on him. If you use the muzzle the dog cannot possibly bite you, and that removes the fear and tension from the training session.

You might wonder if you, the owner, should train your aggressive dog or have a professional do it. Take a step back, take a good look at him, and try to be objective. Ask

**How to Obedience-Train an Aggressive Dog**

yourself this question: "If this weren't my dog, would it be safe enough for me to train him, considering his level of aggression?" If your dog tends to obey and considers you the leader of his pack, and if he is not uncontrollably dangerous, then you are probably right to train him yourself. We feel most aggressive dogs can be trained at home by their owner but . . . *do not attempt to train your dog yourself if he has bitten people, causing them serious injuries. Under these circumstances consult a professional dog trainer who specializes in this area of expertise, or an animal behaviorist, or a veterinarian. If your dog has attacked and injured people, you should seriously consider whether or not to continue living with him.*

Please bear in mind that this training program is not a cure-all. There is no guarantee that your dog will not growl or bite again. With this training course you can at least stop the problem from getting progressively worse. It is important to understand that you never actually change a dog's temperament from aggressive to something else. He will always be an aggressive dog, but you can modify his behavior so that he is controllable and obedient and therefore more enjoyable as a pet. If your dog is obedience-trained, you will be able to stop him and prevent unwanted behavior when he attempts to behave aggressively. For example, a well-trained dog will not lunge at people or other dogs if he is commanded to walk in "Heel" properly and is corrected if he doesn't obey. If your dog is not allowed on your bed in the first place and is placed in a "Stay" position, then he cannot bite you when you shoo him off, and so on. This training course will give you the knowledge, the tools, and the skills to take charge of your aggressive dog and allow you to enjoy him more than ever before.

If your dog was previously trained but continues to plague you with aggressive-behavior problems, train him again. Start at the very beginning of this course. Many dog owners believe their dog is trained even though he may "Sit" on command only some of the time or may walk in the proper "Heel" position only until he sees another dog. Dogs that come to you on command only some of the time or lie down whenever they want to or never listen to their owners should not be considered trained dogs. The best thing to do is start the training process over again. When training an aggressive dog, there is no room for mistakes.

Before starting out you must consider what motivates your shy or aggressive dog to pay attention. Will he work for your praise, his ball, his toys, his Frisbee, food rewards? Dog training requires you to reward your dog after each and every correction. The best reward is verbal praise. However, some dogs must be motivated differently to get past their behavior problems and perform properly, and that's where these special rewards fit in. You will learn when and how to use special rewards as you continue. Using training motivators such as food strengthens the bond between you and your dog and helps to establish the dog's trust in what you are trying to do with him.

In dog training, people lead and dogs follow. To accomplish this, you must establish a relationship based on love, kindness, and leadership. Learn to exercise gentle persistence, patience, and understanding.

Understanding the basics of natural dog behavior

helps a great deal in training, especially if your dog is aggressive. See chapter 2, "How Did He Get That Way?" An aggressive dog needs leadership and authority from the person training him. All wolf packs require a leader to ensure their survival, which is a concept genetically programmed into their natural behavior.

Every dog expects someone in his pack (or family) to be the leader. He becomes insecure until *someone* takes charge. An aggressive dog will take over as leader of the pack if no one else does. Dog training becomes much easier when you understand that your dog will obey commands from any member of the family with a dominant personality or from those who exhibit a take-charge attitude. Once you become the leader of the pack from the dog's point of view, he will accept your authority for the rest of his life.

It is essential that all members of a family take a dominant position over the family dog. That does not mean being physically or emotionally abusive. For example, your hands must only be used for petting and for expressions of affection, not for hitting. Hollering and shouting and physical punishment are useless as training techniques, damage the bond with him, and are just plain unkind. Towering over a small dog and handling him roughly are intimidating actions and frighten him. Pointing a threatening, accusing finger at a dog when scolding him has a very negative impact. All dogs need to feel that they are accepted members of the family. That is why they have such a strong desire to please. You *can* be dominant with the family dog and still be playful and happy in day-to-day activities with him. When you truly bond with your dog, your attitude toward him will be as loving as it is fun.

You can be the person in charge and still be cheerful and affectionate.

Obedience training is based on a dog's acceptance of the humans' position of dominance and his willingness to be a subordinate member of the family. All dogs thrive on being accepted as part of the family because it is simply a substitute dog pack from their point of view. Just like the pack, the family offers a dog survival and comfort, and the price for this is his acceptance of the ranking order, which explains his desire to please. In dog training there are established methods of teaching dogs the mechanical means of carrying out the various obedience commands, such as "Sit," "Stay," "Heel," and so on, all of which are taught in this chapter.

## Praise and Correction

The most important dog-training tool available is the concept of "praise and correction." *Praise,* which is your dog's reward for doing the right thing, is usually given in the form of an enthusiastic compliment, such as, "Good boy! What a good dog!" Sometimes it is a pat on the body. Food tidbits are often useful as a reward for exceptionally stubborn, fearful, or aggressive behavior. For most dogs praise is the most powerful motivation for learning. It tells them that you are pleased and reinforces the teaching of each command. Praise may be given lavishly but should not be squandered. When training your aggressive dog, be certain he has really earned his reward. That will make him work harder for your approval.

It is of vital importance to understand that *every time you praise your dog, you are teaching him to do whatever he did just before the praise was given.* This can work against you if you praise a dog immediately after he behaves aggressively or unacceptably. This most often happens when a dog owner tries to calm a dog down or soothe him after he has done something wrong. If you say "Good boy" in order to quiet the dog after barking, you are in effect teaching him to bark and to repeat what he just did. "Good boy" in that context is a reward for barking.

A *correction* is a signal to the dog that he either did not obey a command or failed to execute it properly. The traditional correction is a snap of the leash, which is attached to a training collar (also known as a "choke collar"). This communicates a negative message because it is usually accompanied by a firm sounding "No!" from the trainer.

There must never be any pain or abuse connected with this gesture. It is simply a means of communicating to the dog that he did the wrong thing. In this training course you will be advised to use a shake can (an empty soda can with pennies inside) or a spray bottle of water for this purpose. Do not misuse these tools. A dog must never associate corrections with punishment. A correction is a teaching tool. Punishment is not effective for teaching anything, nor is it humane. Punishment creates more aggressive behavior than it changes and defeats the purpose of the training, which is to get your dog under control. If you learn when and how to praise or correct your dog effectively, you will have at your fingertips the primary means of communicating with him. *Praise* and *correction* are how you tell your dog what is right and what is wrong.

The goal of obedience training is to get your dog to behave in a specific way each time you give him a command. This is accomplished by creating a line of communication that is based on what you have taught him. When he fails to obey, he must be reminded that he *must* obey the command. The reminders are praise and correction.

Try not to lose your temper when the dog frustrates you. This can be for your own safety as well as for training him effectively. Control your voice so it sounds firm and demanding. Do not be harsh. Learn to coax a sensitive dog instead of being severe with him. Develop an upbeat, happy tone of voice instead of one that sounds hysterical. *Bear in mind that you must first teach a dog what you want before you can expect him to do it.* If your dog does not obey your commands, it is probably because you have not taught him the specifics of the command properly.

As your dog's trainer you must always be self-assured, easygoing, patient, and, most important of all, calm. Allow your attitude to express the opposite of your dog's disposition. If he is aggressive, you should be neutral. You cannot stop his aggression during training by being aggressive yourself. There is an important difference between being aggressive and being assertive.

Obviously, training a puppy is very different from training a grown dog. Puppies require a more gentle, patient manner because of their easily injured bodies and their easily bruised egos. Grown dogs require a more demanding manner, unless they are shy, unusually sensitive, or aggressive to the extreme. Puppies require shorter lessons. Your demands on a puppy should not be the same as those on an older dog. You must be more tolerant and expect mistakes and a bit of mischief.

# The Obedience Commands in This Course

**Sit.** On command, the dog sits erect with all his weight on his haunches. "Sit" involves a verbal command.

**Heel.** This is on-leash control of the dog when out walking with him. The dog walks on your left side with his head next to your thigh. He should walk when you walk and stop when you do. When you speed up, the dog should speed up. This helps when you are in traffic, crossing the street, or trying to catch up with a friend. When you both stop, the dog should "Sit" next to you as a learned part of the command. "Heel" involves a verbal command and specific leash techniques.

**Stay.** The dog remains in whatever position you place him ("Sit-Stay" or "Down-Stay") until he is released from the command. Getting your dog to "Sit" is of no use unless the dog has been trained to hold the position until you release him from it. "Stay" involves a verbal command and a hand signal.

**Down.** The dog is on the ground, head erect, eyes looking forward. His front legs are extended and the hind legs relaxed with the rear weight resting on both haunches. The dog's stomach should be flat on the ground. "Down" involves a verbal command and a hand signal. If the dog is well trained he can execute the command with a hand signal only.

**Come When Called.** The dog comes to you when you call him and goes into a "Sit" position facing you and waits for your next command. This is used when you need a dog to come to you for any reason at all, such as putting his collar on his neck. "Come When Called" involves a verbal command and a hand signal.

**Place.** At your command the dog stops whatever he is doing and leaves wherever he is doing it, goes to a designated place (such as a corner of the room), and stays there after commanded to "Stay." "Place" involves a verbal command only.

These are the basic obedience commands that must be taught if a family is going to have control over their aggressive dog's actions and behavior. Dog training for any dog, but especially an aggressive one, is not a luxury, it is a necessity. Big dogs, little dogs, purebred dogs, or mixed breeds all need to be trained. There are many professionals available throughout the United States who are no further away than the Yellow Pages if you decide you cannot or should not do it yourself. No matter how it is accomplished, obedience-training an aggressive dog is the only way to get him under control. It is impossible to solve any specific aggressive-behavior problems, as detailed in chapter 5, "Solving Your Dog's Aggressive-Behavior Problems," without first obedience-training your dog. Once he is under control with the help of this chapter, your relationship with your dog, with your family, and with your neighbors will be greatly improved.

## Important Training Tips

1.  Only one person should be the dog's teacher throughout the obedience course. Once the dog is trained, other members of the household can then learn how to execute the commands.
2.  Assuming your dog is not food-aggressive, do not feed him two or three hours before each

training session. It is much easier to train a dog if he is hungry. He will be more inclined to follow you and do anything for you. If he is hungry, you are going to be the most important person in his life and he will learn the commands you are teaching more readily with the promise of being fed.

3. Select a place to train your dog that has no distractions. That means no other dogs or people or activities should be present. Otherwise your dog will not be able to concentrate. A secluded training area is good for the trainer as well. Many people training a dog for the first time find it difficult to perform the necessary tasks in front of other people. They become inhibited.

4. Unless otherwise instructed, do not obedience-train an aggressive dog in his own territory, which means in your home, your yard, or any other place he occupies. Take him to a place he is not compelled to defend. This is especially important for dominant-aggressive dogs and territorial/overprotective–aggressive dogs.

5. Do not train an aggressive dog in a small, confined area, because it can frighten him and make him behave aggressively.

6. Try to train your dog in short sessions, at least twice a day.

7. When training your dog, do not use negative body language. Do not kneel over him in an overpowering way, especially if the dog is frightened or cornered. Do not make sudden

movements or gestures that make your dog jittery and nervous.

8. Be aware of your dog's body language, which will tell you if he is fearful or dominant and help you decide which of the teaching techniques to use for each command. Your dog's body language will also guide you into the best frame of mind for relating to your dog effectively. Dominant body language includes a stiffened trunk, erect ears, rigid, unmoving tail, raised hairs on the back, neck, and tail, and an attempt to stare directly at your eyes. Fearful body language includes flattened ears, tail lowered or curled between the legs, cringing, or shaking. A fear-aggressive dog may display both fear and dominant body language. If this behavior is seen, it is best to stop training or place a soft nylon muzzle on the dog, as described in "Training Equipment," below, and continue.

9. Be aware of your dog's facial expressions while training him. Dominant-aggressive behavior can be seen in such facial expressions as curled lips, exposed teeth, corners of the mouth drawn forward, and a wrinkled nose. Many of these expressions are seen in a fear-aggressive dog as well. Either way, these expressions are warnings of aggressive behavior. In this situation it is best to stop training or to place a soft nylon muzzle on the dog and continue.

10. When you're training an aggressive dog, his name should have only positive associations connected to it. To help achieve this, use his

name when giving all commands. Your dog will enjoy hearing his name, and using it in each command is a positive thing to do. This is contrary to training nonaggressive dogs. In standard dog training, the name is used only with a command that involves forward motion such as "Heel" or "Come When Called," in order to alert the dog. In training an aggressive dog, it is best to say your dog's name before *every* command. It will help him think of the training as a positive experience.

11. After you teach your dog each obedience command, praise him for executing the command properly and correct him when he does not. That definitely places you in a position of authority.

12. Bear in mind that there is no such thing as having your dog trained without your being trained as well. It is essential that you learn to handle the dog properly and how to execute the obedience commands given to the dog. Even if you have a professional train your dog, you still must participate or it just won't work.

13. If your dog growls or snaps at you whenever you try to touch him, cover his mouth with a soft nylon muzzle. Use it before starting each lesson or until you feel safe. The muzzle will allow you to touch the dog and employ the teaching techniques without getting bitten.

14. The key to training your dog effectively is *to teach, to show, to praise,* and *to love* him.

## Training Equipment

### Leashes

To train a dog you need a six-foot leather leash of good quality so there can never be any possibility of its breaking while outdoors. Dogs are strong and they pull hard, so the leash must be dependable. A leather leash, five-eighths of an inch or three-fourths of an inch wide is the most useful and durable type for training and everyday use and is ideal for medium-to-large dogs. You will also use it for solving most of your dog's aggressive-behavior problems. Small dogs require a narrower-width leather leash, such as half-inch or less. Strength and comfort are the goals when selecting a leash. Ornate and colorful leashes may look chic, but you must be certain they will not break while you have your dog outdoors near traffic.

Part of this course calls for a fifteen-foot training leash made of thick canvas. It is available in most pet-supply stores and through mail-order catalogs. You may have to compromise with a thirty-foot training leash if that is all that is available.

### Training Collars

The leash is useless unless it is attached to a collar around the dog's neck. Training collars serve a more important purpose than providing a place on which to hook the leash. They are quite different from typical leather collars with metal buckles. Training collars are designed to tighten and instantly loosen around the dog's neck in order to communicate to him that he did the wrong thing.

You will need a metal or a nylon training collar. This is also referred to as a "choke collar." It consists of a short length of chain or nylon with a large, metal ring at each end. The most comfortable and reliable chain collars are made of smooth, jewel-like links that are welded together for strength. To get the right fit, measure the diameter of your dog's neck and purchase a chain or nylon collar that is no more than three inches longer than his neck size. Since collars come in even-numbered sizes, always go to the next larger size. The collar should fit snugly. By looping the chain or the nylon through one of the large rings you form a slipknot that is wide enough to slide over the dog's head and around his neck. The leash can then be snapped onto the outer ring, and it begins to function as one thing, the leash-and-collar.

In some training situations it is important for the collar to ride high on the dog's neck, and only the nylon collar will stay in place. The metal collar tends to slide down. However, because the metal collar tightens and releases quickly and smoothly and affords you more control over the dog if necessary, it is very effective for most training situations. A nylon collar is preferred for puppies and delicate dogs or dogs that are very sensitive. It is also ideal for dogs with long, silky fur, to avoid damaging the coat.

We do not recommend the use of pronged metal choke collars, because it is too easy for nonprofessionals to misuse them, in which case they can injure a dog. Nor do we recommend electric collars, because they represent a form of shock therapy rather than dog training. Far greater results can be achieved with the proper use of conventional training techniques and equipment. We believe electric shocks are painful, upsetting, and scare dogs into submission. It is also impossible to foretell what the short-term and long-term negative behavioral effects of shocks will be from dog to dog. The use of shock collars can be especially unpredictable when used on aggressive dogs. Besides, why would anyone send electric shocks into a good friend's body?

## Soft Nylon Muzzle

*When used properly* a dog muzzle is one of the most useful training aids available. If your aggressive dog growls when you touch him or has nipped or snapped at or bitten you or anyone else, it is important to use a muzzle when training him. Because of its flexibility and featherweight quality, we recommend a soft nylon muzzle with an adjustable strap and quick-release buckle. Some nylon muzzles have Velcro fasteners for instant on-off ease. There is also a nylon muzzle available with wide fabric sides that permit a dog to pant and move with comfort and a sturdy

**How to Obedience-Train an Aggressive Dog**

mesh panel, which helps to circulate air. There are also leather muzzles that cover the dog's entire snout; we do not recommend them as they are not as comfortable for the dog and can be more difficult to get on and off.

Make sure you buy a muzzle that is the right size for your dog. Adjust the straps so your dog will be as comfortable as possible. When using the soft muzzle, you will have to get your dog accustomed to wearing it. Do this before using it in the training sessions. Put it on and take it off ten or fifteen times for several days, praising the dog each time you do this. Use a soft tone of voice and touch the dog lovingly when you do anything with the muzzle off. Some dogs resist this equipment the first few times but eventually accept it as they get used to it. The dog must learn to accept wearing this equipment just like he did the leash and collar.

Never leave a muzzle on a dog longer than necessary, as it could be life threatening. A dog's body relies on his unrestricted ability to pant as part of his system for lowering body temperature. A muzzle left on too long can limit the dog's ability to open his mouth and thus cool himself with the tongue. Consider the muzzle a short-term, temporary training tool that should not be used for every dog.

If your dog is very aggressive and threatening, you will always be safe if you place the muzzle on for each training session. You may remove the muzzle when each lesson is over. Never leave a dog alone with a muzzle covering his mouth. If you do not watch him while the muzzle is on, he could work it around with his paws and have breathing difficulties.

## Correction Tools

**Spray Bottle.** A spray bottle filled with water makes an excellent correction tool for unruly, aggressive dogs. A plant sprayer is fine for this purpose. This is very effective when the dog is not wearing his leash and collar and you cannot administer a leash correction. Keep the spray bottle filled with water and keep it in a convenient location, such as on a table or mantel. More than one spray bottle located around the house is even more efficient. When the dog misbehaves, reach for the spray bottle and gently spray water in the dog's face and say, "No!" in a firm tone of voice. This should stop the misbehaving. Immediately follow the correction with a praising statement, such as, "Good boy."

**Shake Can.** A shake can is easy to make and very effective, especially when the dog is not wearing his leash and collar. Take an empty soda or juice can, wash it, and slip ten pennies into it. Tape the opening closed so the pennies cannot fall out. Shake the can up and down. It will make a very loud, compelling racket. This is an excellent tool for correcting a dog, especially a puppy. It easily gets his attention when shaken loudly and accompanied with a firm "No!" This should stop the misbehaving. Immediately follow the correction with praise for having stopped. This is an important aspect of all corrections.

### Motivators

Some shy, frightened, or extremely aggressive dogs are uncooperative and difficult to train. Motivators are a wonderful option for dogs with extreme behavior. Food treats, for example, are very effective for dogs whose aggression makes it impossible to conduct a training session. The same is true for dogs that hide from you. You can get past these sort of obstacles by capturing their interest with something they like or enjoy. Try using snacks, tidbits, or food treats as rewards and other inducements if needed during training sessions. You can use chew-toys, toss-toys, tug-toys, or balls for this purpose. You won't need all of these. Just select the one or two motivators that work best for your dog. Bear in mind that the best reward is your verbal praise, and it is the motivator of choice.

### You

Of all the equipment necessary for obedience training, there is none more important, more useful, or more effective than the various components that are the sum total of you. Aspects of your body are among the most important training tools available, and they cost nothing. The importance of your attitude, your behavior, your handling techniques, and your good intentions cannot be emphasized enough. On the one hand you must be the dog's leader, but on the other hand you must also be a kind, patient teacher.

**Your Voice.** A proper tone of voice and the words you use are extremely important to the success of training a dog. Dogs respond well to commands spoken clearly in a firm tone of voice. The sound of your voice makes the difference in having the dog accept your authority or not. You must not make a squeaking sound in a soft tone of voice when giving a command. Neither can you scream or holler, which almost always leads to endless repetition of the command. Poor enunciation of the command words also gets little or no response. You can get your dog's attention only by producing a resonant, authoritative sound, which is necessary for giving commands and vocal corrections.

**Your Body.** Dogs are very responsive to their owners' body language, for better or worse. An aggressive dog will not be totally obedient, if at all, to a human with a loose grip on the leash or a slouched-over body that seems weak or submissive. This only encourages an aggressive dog to lead, with the human following. Holding a leash properly with firmness while walking the dog improves the situation. Keep your body straight and move in a brisk and determined manner. Do not be overbearing, however, with a shy or fear-aggressive dog or with a puppy. Overpowering such dogs with a loud voice or with dominant body language gets negative results. Try not to tower over a puppy or very small dog by standing too close. Little dogs and some shy dogs need a little more distance from their trainers and handler to abate their fears. When possible, kneel down to their level, eye to eye, and speak gently. Use common sense and tailor your voice and body to the needs of the dog.

## How to Use the Training Collar and Leash

Allow the chain-link collar to hang down in a vertical position with one hand on the top ring and the other on the bottom ring. Let the chain drop through the bottom ring so that it forms a loop while you still hold the top ring with your other hand. Place the dog's head through the newly formed loop with the top ring pointing to the dog's right as you extend it from the body. It is important to slip the proper side of the collar over the dog's head. When placing the loop over the dog's head, it is correct if it looks like the letter "P" around the neck. When incorrect, the loop looks like the number "9" and will not tighten and release as it should. When the leash is pulled taut, it must allow the collar to smoothly tighten around the dog's neck. If it is on the dog correctly, it should slide easily and quickly to its original position once you release the tension on the leash.

Next, attach the metal clip of the leash to the outer

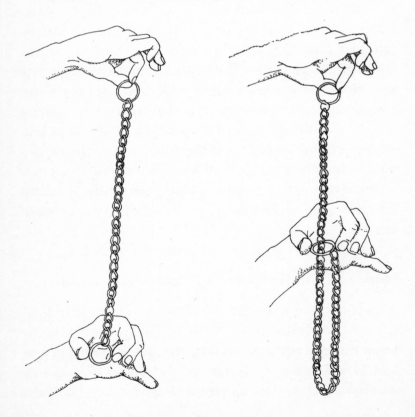

ring of the collar. Always stand on the dog's right side for the sake of consistency and face the same direction as the dog. Allow the leash to drape across your legs and hold your right hand open, thumb up. Place the sewn loop at the end of the leash over the thumb of your right hand as if it were hanging on a hook. With the leash lying across your open palm, gather up the slack from the middle, place it, too, into your right hand so that there is a second loop over your thumb and much less leash lying across your knees. The folded straps of the leash are now lying across the palm of your right hand. Close your hand so that you have a firm grip on the gathered leash with your fingernails facing you. Adjust the length of the leash so that it crosses no more than the width of your body, allowing just a bit of slack.

For greater security, also place your left hand around the leash straps, just under your right hand, as though you were holding a baseball bat. Both hands should hold the leash, but with the fingernails of your left hand facing away from your body, in the opposite direction of your right hand. This makes your grip as secure as possible when jerking the leash for a correction or when walking in "Heel." If you are of average height, only two or three feet of slack should be draped from the dog's collar, across your knees, and into both your hands. You are now ready to give your dog a leash correction.

## How to Execute a Leash Correction

Make sure the training collar is around the dog's neck so that it forms the letter "P" and tightens and releases smoothly and efficiently. With the leash attached to the

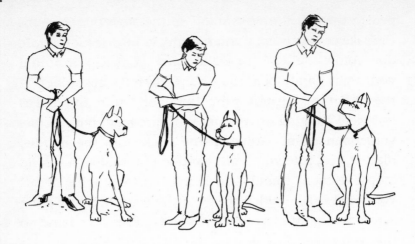

extended ring of the collar gently test it for proper movement. It must tighten around the dog's neck when the
leash is pulled and loosen instantly when released.

To perform a leash correction, jerk or snap the leash
quickly toward your right side and in an upward direction, away from the outside of your right thigh. If you do
it properly, the dog will experience a mild sensation. As
you jerk the leash, say "No!" in a firm tone of voice. This
will communicate to him that he has not performed properly. The jerking motion of the leash must not be given so
hard as to knock the dog off his feet. But it must be firm
enough to tighten the training collar, delivering a mild
sensation. Actually, the snapping sound of the metal links
has more corrective value than the tightened feeling
around the dog's neck. For this reason there is no need to
jerk the leash too hard.

Release the tension immediately after snapping the
leash so the collar does not stay tightened around the dog's

neck for longer than a split second. Immediately after each leash correction, praise the dog in a happy, friendly tone of voice. Say, "Good dog!" It communicates to him that everything is all right between you and that he did the right thing by accepting the correction. *This is very important.* All corrections require two components: a negative reinforcement and a positive reinforcement. The negative is the snap of the leash, which tells the dog he did something wrong or incorrectly. The positive reinforcement is the friendly praise, which is a reward to the dog for accepting the correction and improving his performance.

You can practice the snapping motion of the correction by placing the training collar around your left wrist and pretending it is the dog's neck. Do everything as described so that you get a sense of how hard to pull the leash in a correction without hurting the dog. Do not become overzealous. Never correct your dog unless it is necessary. Too many corrections will ruin the effectiveness of the technique and make him leash-shy.

It is essential to understand that not every dog is the same. They vary in temperament and therefore require different approaches to leash corrections depending on their age, size, sensitivity, and temperament. Common sense should dictate how firmly or how softly to administer your corrections. In each section dealing with a specific training command, you will be guided as to how hard or soft to be when correcting the dog, based on his type of aggression.

Never correct your dog while you are teaching him the basics of a command. However, once he has demonstrated that he has learned the command, it is fair to correct him if he refuses to obey or makes a mistake. In dog training, he must respond on command. If he does not respond properly, the dog owner should administer a reminder using the leash correction. That is negative reinforcement.

To review the leash correction: Jerk the leash quickly and firmly *upward* and to the *right* when he refuses to obey or makes a mistake. As you do this, say "No!" in a firm tone of voice. Release the tension on the leash instantly and then praise the dog lovingly. That is a proper leash correction.

## Getting Your Dog's Attention with "No" and "Okay"

Getting your dog's attention and keeping it are crucial to training an aggressive dog. Good use of your voice and proper body language are the keys to achieving the successful control of your dog. When training a dog, the dominant/subordinate relationship is of primary concern. You, the dog owner, must become the leader of the pack; your voice must be firm and resonant when you give obedience commands (especially during the training sessions). You must maintain a no-nonsense attitude, as if you were teaching algebra to junior high school students. If you do your part, your dog will do his part. Remember, his willingness to obey your commands goes a long way toward altering his aggressive behavior and just may spare him from losing his home.

Think of your family as your dog's pack and of yourself as the leader of his pack. You must consider your dog subordinate to you. This doesn't require an overbearing or abusive manner. Hollering at or hitting an aggressive dog can be dangerous, and it certainly will not make him less aggressive. Good teachers make it clear that they are in charge without having to raise their voices or make threats. If you do not feel like a pack leader, then fake it. Think of it as acting.

Learn to exclaim "No!" in a loud, firm tone of voice when necessary. "No!" is the most authoritative and negative word in any language. It is easy to use this term as a corrective tool by firmly establishing its use exclusively for when your dog makes a mistake. Use the word, all by itself, as a tool. This is essential. Your reprimanding "No!" should be a firm, vocal sound that comes from deep within your stomach. Once you've established that your "No!" means no, be consistent. Never back down. Remember this: Dogs do not understand words unless they are associated with specific emphasis and tone of voice. The sounds you make and the words you use are essential tools for training. Dogs respond instantly to simple commands containing a minimum of words, spoken clearly in a firm tone of voice.

In order to produce a firmer-sounding tone, here is something to practice. Take in a deep breath, inhaling so that air enters your stomach and you can feel your waist expand. Let it out slowly with the use of your stomach muscles. As you slowly release the air, say "No" in an exaggerated way. You will notice that your voice becomes deeper and your tone has much more authority to it. Practice this simple exercise alone as often as you can. It will definitely help.

You must be able to exaggerate the sound of your voice in order to teach your dog right from wrong. Modify your vocal pitch and tone so that there is a great difference between an enthusiastic and loving "Good dog" and an authoritative "Down."

The two most important words used to communicate with a dog are "No!" and "Okay." "No!" is used to stop him when he misbehaves or does not perform correctly. Use it consistently to indicate your disapproval; don't confuse him with other words, such as "Stop it" or "Don't you do it." It is equally important not to associate your dog's name with the negativism of "No." For this reason, never say, "Jocasta, no!" When a dog hears his name, he should have a happy association with it. Do not repeat a command word to get a response. Your dog should obey "No!" the first time you say it. If you have to repeat it over and over, you diminish your credibility as the leader. If your dog does not obey the command, administer a mild leash correction as you say, "No! Good boy."

The word "Okay" is a positive command of anticipation or release. Use it as an upbeat prefix to your dog's name. Say, "Okay, Thunder, come!" Say the word "Okay" with an ascending, happy sound, immediately followed by "Thunder, come!" You should also use it as a release from training sessions or as a release from walking in the "Heel" position so that he can relieve himself in the street. Saying "Okay" in an upbeat tone of voice is like saying "Class dismissed!" "Okay" should have a pleasant association for your dog and should never be used negatively.

## Using the Obedience Commands

### Sit

**Performance:** After you give the verbal command "Sit," your dog must lower his buttocks to the ground, with his hind legs tucked underneath. His front legs should be extended in a straight, upright position as he remains attentive, waiting for your next command.

[*Note: If your dog growls or snaps at you whenever you try to touch him or approach him, cover his mouth with a soft nylon muzzle, as described in "Training Equipment," above. Use it before starting each lesson or until you feel safe. The muzzle will allow you to touch the dog and employ the teaching techniques without getting bitten.*]

Two techniques are offered in this course for teaching "Sit." Although there are other techniques, these two are the most appropriate. The first is the *Motivation Technique,* which is best for dogs that are generally aggressive and difficult to manage. The second is the *Placing Technique,* which is best for dogs that are aggressive in only a few situations and manageable most other times. Read both techniques before deciding which one is best for your dog.

You will need a training collar and a six-foot leather leash for both techniques. Place them on the dog as described above in "How to Use the Training Collar and Leash."

**The Motivation Technique.** This is the best technique to use for an aggressive dog or one that refuses to cooperate in the teaching process for any reason. The goals here are to gain the dog's confidence and entice him into working as well as to avoid getting bitten. Select a motivator you think will work best, such as a food treat he really likes or one of the toys he enjoys. *Do not use food as a motivator for a possessive-aggressive dog for whom food is the issue.* The motivator of choice is used to capture the dog's interest, to keep him focused on the lesson, and to manipulate him into moving into the proper position for the command "Sit."

Use a firm but nonthreatening tone of voice for an aggressive dog. Do not present a threat by towering over him or standing too close. Do not make direct eye contact. In dog behavior a direct stare is a challenge for dominance. Be cautious and do not make sudden, jerky motions with your body, particularly with your hands. Stroke the dog with affection if he'll let you and reassure him with a soothing tone of voice.

If your dog is average size, stand about two feet in front of him. Hold the leash with your right hand and gather it up, leaving approximately twelve inches stretched above his head with no slack. Have the motivator in your left hand. (If you are left-handed, reverse the hands.) Show the dog the motivator at eye level. Bring it close to his nose and then move it upward slowly past his eyes. As the food or toy passes his eyes, say, "Mike, Sit," and continue pulling up on the leash with pressure in a steady, even-flowing motion. Say the command in a firm tone of voice, stretching out the word "Sit" so that the sound continues until he is in the proper position.

The dog should be keenly focused on the food or toy as the pull of the leash compels him to go into a "Sit" position in order to be comfortable without losing sight of what's in your left hand. The instant he sits, lavish him with exuberant praise and give him the food treat or the toy. Repeat this procedure ten or fifteen times until the dog makes the connection between going into the "Sit" position and getting the reward. The next step is to try going through the procedure by just giving the verbal command and without using the motivator. At this point your lavish praise should be sufficient reward for executing the command properly. Do not correct the dog for failing to obey until you are certain he has learned the command.

When using food to motivate him, give him only a small piece each time. It should not be a full-size snack but rather a taste reward. To give him the food without getting hurt, close your hand and make a fist. Hold the food in the cavity created between your little finger and your palm so only a portion shows. This will prevent the dog from nipping your skin.

Disregard "The Placing Technique," below, and move on to "For Both Teaching Techniques," which is the end of the lesson.

**The Placing Technique.** This technique is recommended for dogs that are aggressive in some but not all situations. It is also ideal for frightened dogs, because you do not stand over them; instead, you must place yourself at eye level. Also, you do *not* apply downward pressure with your hand on the dog's rump.

With this technique you have the option of kneeling next to the dog, bending over him, or standing next to him if he is very large. It depends on the dog's size and how close he'll allow you to get.

Stand next to, bend over, or kneel at the right side of the dog so that you have access to his hind legs. Hold the leash in your right hand approximately twelve inches above the dog's head and gently place your left hand behind the dog's rear legs at the first joint beneath the rump, which is similar to where the knee is on humans. These joints bend forward when the dog sits. Place the palm of your hand upward as though the dog were going to sit on it.

Say, "Mike, Sit," in a firm tone of voice. Stretch out the word "Sit" so that the sound continues until he is in the proper position. As you give the command, bend his rear legs forward at the joint by pushing them with the edge of your left hand. This makes the legs gently collapse forward in a natural, easy manner. As you do this, pull the leash upward with your right hand until it is taut but not uncomfortable for the dog. These actions will move him into the correct "Sit" position. Remove your left hand quickly

just before his rump touches the ground. Praise him enthusiastically as he moves into the correct position. Repeat this action ten or fifteen times. Repetition and praise is how your dog learns each command. Never correct him for mistakes during the teaching process.

**For Both Teaching Techniques.** Give the dog a rest. Allow him to relieve himself, but do not play with him. The training session is not yet over.

After a five-minute rest, repeat the teaching process again ten or fifteen times. You may now correct him if he fails to obey the command. At this time you should not have to use food or push the dog's rear legs forward as you say the command. The dog should go into the proper "Sit" position when given the verbal command and when the leash is pulled above his head. Eventually, the dog will go into a "Sit" position when you simply say the command.

If you give the command and the dog does not obey, administer a leash correction firmly but cautiously. As you jerk the leash, say "No!" in a firm tone of voice.

If your dog is *not generally aggressive,* correct him with a quick, firm jerk of the leash. Praise him immediately after the correction. If he does not go into the proper position, begin the teaching process over.

If your dog *is generally aggressive,* jerk the leash firmly but cautiously and watch for a hostile reaction. You always have the option of using the soft nylon muzzle during the training process if it becomes necessary.

You may now end the lesson, no matter which technique you are using. Always end on a note of success when the dog has accomplished his task well. End the session in a definite manner. Say to the dog, "Okay," slacken the leash, allow him to pee, and then walk him away from the training area in a brisk but positive, congratulatory manner. Your dog may want a walk, or he may be tired and simply desire to go home and take a nap. Repeat this procedure every day for six days. Practice sessions are important before moving on to the next command.

## Sit-Stay

**Performance:** The dog must remain in a proper "Sit" position until you release him from the "Stay" command.

[*Note: If your dog growls or snaps at you whenever you try to touch him or approach him, cover his mouth with a soft nylon muzzle, as described in "Training Equipment," above. Use it before starting each lesson or until you feel safe. The muzzle will allow you to touch the dog and employ the teaching techniques without getting bitten.*]

Unlike with most other commands, you may teach this lesson on the dog's home territory because there is nothing threatening about it. However, teach the command in an open space and not in a crowded area, so that he does not ever feel cornered. When an aggressive dog is cornered he growls, which is a warning that he will lunge at you or bite. This defeats the purpose of the training, which is to convince him that you are the dominant one. Your dog should not feel restricted in the training area. However, do not allow other dogs or other people in the training location.

Be careful with your hand movements. Your dog may be hand-shy. If he has ever been hit or yelled at, the hand signal used in this command could instigate a serious bite. Refer to "The Punishment-Reaction Test" in chapter 3,

"How Aggressive *Is* Your Dog? Tests and Signs of Aggression." If your dog is hand-shy, recondition him in the following manner: Hold a piece of food in your hand and get his attention on it. Move it around his face, his nose, and finally above his head. After doing this for a while, and after allowing the dog to have the treat once or twice, bring your hand down and *pretend* to hit him. Give him the treat. Do this as often as necessary until the dog no longer flinches when you make the hitting gesture with your hand — the difference being, of course, that your hand gives him the food. If you repeat this action often, he will soon associate your hand movements with something he likes and become at ease with them, especially when you teach the hand signal for this command.

If your dog is fear-aggressive or dominant-aggressive, be cautious with your body language. In order to avoid an aggressive reaction, do not lean over such a dog. Simply being aware of this will keep you from moving improperly when teaching this command.

Use the dog's name before saying the command word in order to get his attention and to make the lesson fun for him. Dogs usually perk up and enjoy hearing their name: "Mike, Stay." For a generally aggressive dog, your tone of voice should be firm but nonthreatening. A shy or fearful dog requires a soft, soothing tone of voice. For any other temperament type, use a firm but not harsh tone of voice.

At your discretion you may use motivators, such as food treats or toys, if your dog resists this command, but they are not necessary for most dogs. If he loves his tennis ball, it is acceptable to give him the "Sit" and "Stay" commands with the ball in his mouth. The idea is to make the lesson as pleasant as possible while getting him to learn.

**How to Obedience-Train an Aggressive Dog**

The success of this command could significantly diminish his aggressive behavior.

**The Technique.** Always have the dog successfully execute the command he learned in the previous session before teaching a new command. It will sharpen his attention and start him out in a positive frame of mind. Once you congratulate him for performing properly, he will be well motivated for the next lesson. "Sit-Stay" involves a verbal command, a hand signal, and a special, pivotal turning motion. To teach this command you will need the training collar, a six-foot leather leash, and a fifteen-foot training leash.

Place the training collar around your dog's neck and hook the leash to it. Have the dog stand next to you on your left side as you both face the same direction. Hold the leash in your right hand, in the manner outlined on page 113, with two or three feet draped across your knees. Give him the command "Sit." Praise your dog for obeying your command. *Remember, you must always praise your dog after every command or correction.* If the dog does not obey the command or has forgotten the command, give him a reminder with a leash correction, as you say "No!" and then "Good boy." If he still does not get into the right position, give him the command again and repeat the teaching steps for "Sit." Do not forget the praise.

Once the dog has assumed the correct "Sit" position, give him the verbal command "Mike, Stay" and use the hand signal. Praise him.

**The Hand Signal.** Be cautious when teaching the hand signal, especially if your dog is hand-shy. Refer to the in-

formation about this provided above in the introductory section to this command.

Flatten your left hand and hold it vertically in front of the dog's face with the palm turned toward his eyes. Hold your hand approximately three or four inches from his eyes. It is exactly the same hand signal as for stopping when driving a car. If the dog moves, correct him with the leash, saying "No!" followed with praise. Do not say anything extraneous while teaching this command. The dog should be sharply focused on you as he concentrates on what you are teaching him. You may repeat the command "Mike, Stay" in a soft tone of voice if he looks restless. Praise him again in a subdued manner.

**The Pivotal Turn.** Hold the leash straight up, above the dog's head about twelve or eighteen inches. Next, turn

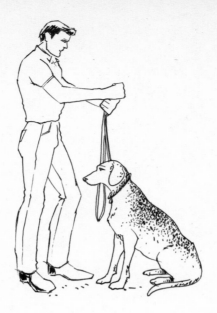

around and face him while keeping him in the "Stay" position. The turn you make is unique and designed to avoid stimulating the dog into moving.

As you turn to face the dog, swivel on the ball of your left foot, which stays in place. Slowly move your right foot into a position that allows you to stand in front of the dog. Once you are standing in front of the dog on your right foot, bring your left foot next to it. You should now be facing the dog, holding him in position with the leash above his head. The leash should remain taut during the entire turning motion. If necessary, keep saying "Mike, Stay" as you make the turn, but say it in a quiet, soothing tone of voice. Praise him but not too exuberantly. If the dog tries to leave his position, say "Stay," praise him, and start again. Praise the dog for holding the position once you are standing in front of him, even if you had to correct him or hold him in place with the leash. The idea is to motivate the dog to obey with praise. That is his reward. The important teaching element is your leash control and the sound of your voice as you move. Repeat this procedure ten times, holding the dog in the "Stay" position for fifteen seconds after each pivotal turn. Take a break for five minutes and allow the dog to pee.

**Stepping Back.** Repeat everything you did from the beginning. Give the dog the verbal command and the hand signal. Praise him. While standing in front of him but back a few paces, allow the leash to extend but always in a taut, upward position. The dog will probably try to move toward you. Say "No!" in a firm tone of voice and quickly

**How to Obedience-Train an Aggressive Dog**

return to your position in front of the dog. Praise him and repeat the command "Mike, Stay" using the hand signal. Again, back away a few paces. Keep repeating the command "Stay" in a subdued tone of voice, praising him immediately after."

Starting from the very beginning of the command at the dog's side, give him the command "Mike, Stay," use the hand signal, execute the pivotal turn, praise the dog, hold the position for fifteen seconds, step back a few paces (softly repeating the command), and praise the dog again. Repeat these steps until the dog is able to hold the position for thirty to sixty seconds. Take a five-minute break.

**Using the Entire Leash.** Repeat everything detailed above but instead of stepping back a few paces, step back until the entire leash is stretched out, keeping it taut. If the dog tries to leave the position, say "No!" in a firm tone of voice and move in quickly in front of the dog, holding the leash above his head, praise him, and begin again. Once the dog begins to hold the position, repeat the procedure ten times.

Repeat these procedures with a fifteen-foot training leash (as described in "Training Equipment," above). Increase each step by three-foot increments until you use the entire leash, in order to get more control at a longer distance.

**Walking Halfway Around the Dog.** *Do not teach this part of the technique until the dog has held the position with the full fifteen-foot leash extended in front of him. Otherwise, you may startle him and cause an aggressive reaction.* Repeat everything you've done to this point, but this time try walking halfway around the dog's right side, using the six-foot leash. Once he allows you to do that without leaving his position, try walking around his left side. If he leaves his "Stay" position, say "No!" in a firm tone of voice and start over. Repeat each new phase ten times.

Repeat these procedures with the fifteen-foot training leash. Increase each step by three-foot increments until you use the entire leash, in order to get more control at a longer distance.

**Circling Around the Dog.** *Do not teach this part of the technique until the dog has held the position with the full fifteen-foot leash extended in front of him and you have walked halfway around his right and left sides.* Using the six-foot leash, repeat everything you've done to this point, but this time circle completely around the dog, as you continue to hold him in place. In all probability, he will turn his head in order to follow you with his eyes. This is perfectly acceptable, providing he does not leave his "Stay" position. Repeat the circling action ten times, as you repeat the command "Mike, Stay" in a soothing tone of voice. Keep praising him, especially after completing each circle, but do not praise him with too much exuberance or you will excite him into leaving the position. The session is not yet over.

Repeat these procedures with the fifteen-foot training leash. Increase each step by three-foot increments until you use the entire leash, in order to get more control at a longer distance.

Once you are satisfied he has learned the command "Stay," release him from the session. Say to the dog, "Okay," slacken the leash, allow him to pee, and then walk him away from the training area in a brisk but positive, congratulatory manner. Your dog may want a walk, or he may be tired and simply want to go home and take a nap. Repeat this procedure every day for six days. Practice sessions are important before moving on to the next command.

## HEEL

**Performance:** Your dog must always be at your left side with his head lined up with your leg when walking in "Heel." As you begin to walk, he begins to walk. When you stop, he must stop. If you quicken your pace, so must he.

[*Note: If your dog growls or snaps at you whenever you try to touch him or approach him, cover his mouth with a soft nylon muzzle, as described in "Training Equipment," above. Use it before starting each lesson or until you feel safe. The muzzle will allow you to touch the dog and employ the teaching techniques without getting bitten.*]

The command "Heel" gives you absolute control of your dog when walking him outdoors. This is extremely important in traffic, when crossing the street, or when trying to go directly to a specific place without stopping.

Teaching "Heel" requires a training collar and a six-foot leather leash, a verbal command, and sharp leash technique.

A puppy should be at least three months of age before you attempt to teach him "Heel." Any sooner than this risks impairing his pleasant personality. Even at three months young dogs should be allowed to express their natural curiosity by running ahead to the full extent of the leash. When teaching this command to a very young dog you must be patient and gentle. Be cheerful, energetic, and encouraging. Do not be as demanding as you would be with an adult dog.

When training an adult aggressive dog, praise him on a continual basis as he walks with you in "Heel," after each jerk of the leash, and especially after each successful movement. You cannot give too much praise and encouragement. Being verbal is very important to the teaching process of this command.

Never take your eyes off the dog as you train him. Watch his reaction to every correction you make in order to avoid his potential aggressive behavior. Always praise the dog energetically after giving each command and after every correction. Make the dog enthusiastic about training with your praise.

Your body language should indicate that you are confident and in charge. Do not stare directly into your dog's eyes. That would be taken as a challenge for dominance and could provoke an aggressive act. If you train the dog properly throughout this course, you will slowly but surely develop dominance over him without a confrontation.

Be cautious with the use of your hands. If your dog was ever hit with a bare hand or with an object such as a newspaper, he may snap as you try to touch him. Use your hands slowly and in a nonthreatening manner as they approach his line of sight. Refer to "The Punishment-Reaction Test" in chapter 3, "How Aggressive *Is* Your Dog? Tests and Signs of Aggression" to determine if he is hand-shy.

You can recondition your dog in the following manner: Hold a piece of food in your hand and get his attention focused on it. Move it around his face, his nose, and finally above his head. Give him the treat. After doing this several times, and after allowing the dog to have the treat once or twice, bring your hand down and *pretend* to hit him. Give him the treat. Do this as often as necessary until the dog no longer flinches when you make the hitting gesture with your hand — the difference being, of course, that you never hit him and that your gesture is no longer associated with being hit but rather with a food reward.

Your tone of voice is particularly important when teaching this command. Present a happy, energetic, and encouraging attitude. Your voice can impart the idea that it is fun as well as rewarding to walk properly with you. When giving the command word "Heel" or the correction "No!," use a firm but nonthreatening tone of voice. Never be harsh.

It is very important to teach this command in an area that is quiet, without the distractions of other people or animals. If your dog is very territorial, do not teach him this command at home. Find a place that he does not consider his territory.

Give the dog at least two fifteen-minute sessions a day. Practice walking in "Heel" as often as possible. Take long walks every day and utilize the teaching procedures each time. Practice makes perfect. After the initial teaching session, repeat the procedures for six days, along with the preceding lessons, before teaching a new command.

**The Technique.** Before beginning a new command, have the dog perform what he has been taught to this point. Practice "Sit" and "Sit-Stay." Praise him generously

for carrying out the commands properly. You may now teach "Heel."

The correct position for "Heel" is the dog on your left side with his head next to your knee. Stand next to him, side by side, both facing in the same direction. Hold the leash in your right hand, allowing enough slack so that it drapes across your knees. The verbal command for "Heel" incorporates the use of the dog's name. "Heel" is a forward-motion command, and the dog's name, along with the movement of your left foot, alerts him to that fact.

Give the command "Ziggy, Heel" and start walking with your left foot first. The dog is sure to run ahead of you with a great deal of energy. When he runs to the end of the leash, make a brisk U-turn in a strong manner. This causes a sort of collision and has the effect of jerking the

**How to Obedience-Train an Aggressive Dog**

leash. As you turn, walk in the opposite direction and say, "Ziggy, Heel" in a firm tone of voice. Immediately praise the dog with enthusiasm and encourage him to catch up with you. Keep walking and pat the side of your thigh to get him next to you.

Then turn again, giving the verbal command. Each time you turn, say, "Ziggy, Heel" in a firm tone of voice. Praise him after saying the command and again when he catches up with you, or at least tries to. Be gentler with a younger dog and cautious with one that is aggressive. The beginning of this first "Heel" lesson may be difficult for some dogs. Some resist or become confused. Be patient and understanding.

Continue walking and making U-turns. Maintain a steady march rhythm until the dog catches up. When he does, adjust the length of the leash to the normal two feet across your knees. It is important to talk to your dog, giving him encouragement and praise even though he may be slow or even resist.

[*Some dogs may react aggressively when you jerk the leash as you teach this command. Your dog may try to bite the leash or hold it down with his paws or direct his aggression at you. If your dog has always shown signs of aggressive behavior, such as growling or snarling when you walked with him, or has been a chronic dogfighter, use a motivator for teaching this command. It will reduce the number of times you need to jerk the leash and possibly avoid aggressive reactions while teaching the command.*

*If he loves a particular ball or a toy or is fond of a special food treat, use that as the motivator. Hold the food or the ball in your left hand and lure him with it as you control and guide him with the leash in your right hand. Remember, the goal is to teach the dog to walk reasonably by your side. As you walk, your dog will walk with you and change directions with you without being jerked on the leash. He will simply follow the food in your left hand. Instead of the dog running ahead when first starting out with this command, he will probably focus on the ball or the food and stay with you. In general, the use of a motivator is the best approach for training aggressive dogs. In addition to being an important training aid, it also helps to establish an emotional bond between you and your dog.]*

As you continue to work with the dog, do not be surprised if you occasionally become entangled in the leash when turning. It is more likely to happen when you try a left turn, as you should after a succession of right turns.

To make a left turn, for the first few times do this: Jerk the leash to the right, as in a correction, then say, "Ziggy, Heel," and use your left leg to nudge the dog to the left as you continue to make your left turn. Take a five-minute break. You will both need it. Allow the dog to pee but do not play with him or it will be hard to get him to go back to work.

Begin again from the "Sit-Stay" position, as before. Give the command "Ziggy, Heel" and start off walking with your left foot. It is likely now that your dog will be a bit weary and lag behind. Talk to him and encourage him to keep pace. Your objective should be to keep his attention on you and nowhere else.

Whenever he fails to keep up with you or runs ahead, do the following: Administer a leash correction by gently jerking the leash to the side, say "Ziggy, Heel," make a right turn, and continue to walk in that direction. Praise the dog immediately and gently tap the side of your thigh to encourage him to catch up. The praise keeps the dog informed that you are not angry and that he is now doing the correct thing. By now your leash corrections should be merely reminders of what to do and therefore less intense. Do not overdo it in any case. After fifteen minutes, end the lesson by saying "Okay." Allow the dog to pee and then walk the dog home for a well-deserved rest.

In the second fifteen-minute session of the day, return to the training area. It is time to teach your dog to go into a "Sit" position whenever you come to a full stop.

## Automatic Sit

**Performance:** Your dog goes directly into a proper "Sit" position each time you come to a full stop when walking in "Heel." The dog must stop when you stop and automatically "Sit" without being commanded to do so.

[*Note: If your dog growls or snaps at you whenever you try to touch him or approach him, cover his mouth with a soft nylon muzzle as described in "Training Equipment," above. Use it before starting each lesson or until you feel safe. The muzzle will allow you to touch the dog and employ the teaching techniques without getting bitten.*]

This command is accomplished by alerting the dog that a stop is coming up. The signal for stopping is simply a reduction of your walking speed. If the dog is focused on you, he will be sensitive to any change of pace. As you slow down, so will he.

Before beginning a new command have the dog perform what he has been taught to this point. Practice "Sit," "Sit-Stay," and "Heel." Praise him generously for carrying out the commands properly. You may now teach the "Automatic Sit."

Stand next to your dog, side by side, both facing in the same direction. Hold the leash in your right hand, allowing enough slack so that it drapes across your knees. Place the dog in "Sit" and then "Stay." Give him the command "Ziggy, Heel" and start walking in a forward direction. Make a few right turns, as in a "Heel" but with less intensity. Gradually slow down and then come to a full stop. Give your dog the command "Sit" every time you stop. As you verbally give the command, raise the leash tautly above his head. Assuming he has already learned the command "Sit," that is all that should be necessary. Praise him with great enthusiasm. *If your dog is very aggressive, use a motivator such as food or a toy as before to lure him into a sitting position after giving the command.* Either way, repeat the procedure you are using as many times as it takes to get him to sit without having to say the command. Every time the dog sits on command, give him the praise he deserves and the command "Heel" and start out again. Repeat the procedure to the end of the session.

If the dog does not "Sit" after he has been taught to do so, you may correct him by jerking the leash and saying "No!" in a firm tone of voice immediately followed with praise. If the dog does not respond properly to leash corrections, repeat the teaching techniques for "Sit" until he performs properly.

### Down

**Performance:** On command the dog lowers himself to the ground with his head erect, his eyes looking forward. His front legs are extended and his hind legs relaxed, with the weight of his body resting on both haunches. The dog's stomach lies flat on the ground.

[*Note: If your dog is aggressive or has ever growled or snapped at you, cover his mouth with a soft nylon muzzle as described in "Training Equipment," above. This is especially important for teaching the "Down" command. If necessary, use the muzzle throughout the lesson. It will allow you to teach "Down" without getting bitten.*]

"Down" involves a verbal command and a hand signal. Eventually, the dog is expected to respond to either one separately.

Although all dogs and puppies prefer to lie down when they are tired or bored, "Down" is a difficult command to teach because it requires dogs to be in a submissive position and also makes them feel vulnerable. Dogs often resist the learning process for this command. Aggressive dogs may growl or snap during the teaching process. For this reason, teaching "Down" requires a great deal of repetition, extra time, patience, and effort. The rewards are well worth the added effort, though. A dog that responds properly to the "Down" command is much easier to control and is a pleasure to have in the house.

You are offered four methods here for teaching "Down." Choose only one.

1. *The Paws Technique* involves gently pulling the dog forward with one hand by the front paws into a "Down" position as you give the command. It is the time-honored, most basic technique. It is ideal for the most typical dogs or puppies.

2. *The Foot Technique* involves gently pushing the dog into a "Down" position by applying

pressure to the leash with the bottom of your foot. This technique is most useful for very aggressive dogs (that have a muzzle on). It is also an alternative for dogs that do not respond to the other methods.

3. *The Leg Technique* involves lifting the right or left front leg and moving it forward so as to maneuver the dog into a "Down" position. This method is best for very large dogs whose front paws cannot be held together with one hand or are otherwise difficult to manage.

4. *The Motivator Technique* involves using food treats or a favored toy as a way of luring the dog into the proper "Down" position. This technique is best for stubborn, frightened, or very aggressive dogs, or when all else fails. For some dogs it is the easiest way to teach this command. Do not use food as a motivator, however, for a food-aggressive dog.

All dogs can be taught with these methods, but do not use any of the first three techniques on dogs that growl, snap, or bite unless they are puppies or wearing a soft muzzle.

Please note that these four techniques are only the first part of teaching "Down." After following the instructions for any one of them, you must skip the other three techniques and continue to the remaining procedures involving the hand signal on page 150. This is essential or you will not have taught the command completely.

When you are teaching the "Down" command, some aggressive dogs will try to bite you. To avoid this, be sure your body language is nonthreatening in terms of your gestures and movements. Do not stand over your dog in a way that challenges or intimidates him. Where possible it is best to kneel down alongside him. If you have a reason to be afraid of your dog (such as growling or snapping), be sure to have a soft muzzle on him when kneeling next to him. Do not make direct eye contact. A five-month-old puppy that growls is far less dangerous than an adult dog that growls.

If your dog is hand-shy, be careful with your hand movements. If he has ever been hit or yelled at, the use of your hands in this command could trigger a bite response. Refer to "The Punishment-Reaction Test" in chapter 3, "How Aggressive *Is* Your Dog? Tests and Signs of Aggression." If your dog is hand-shy, recondition him in the following manner: Hold a piece of food in your hand and get his attention fixed on it. Move it around his face, his nose, and finally above his head. Eventually give the dog the treat and praise him enthusiastically. After allowing the dog to have the treat two or three times, bring your hand down with the food in it and *pretend* you are going to hit him. Then give him the treat and the praise. Do this as often as necessary until the dog no longer flinches when you make the pretended hitting gesture with your hand. Give him the food each time you do this along with your enthusiastic praise. If you repeat this action often he will soon become less hand-shy, especially when you use your hands for this command.

Never use your voice in a harsh manner. Your tone should be firm but nonthreatening. If your dog is shy or fearful, use a soft, soothing tone of voice.

Puppies up to six months of age should be corrected

with quick jerks of the leash that are not too hard. Dogs past ten months of age may require harder jerks of the leash, depending on their level of aggressiveness. Adult dogs that require very firm leash corrections should be wearing a soft muzzle to avoid the possibility of your getting bitten.

Teach the dog this command on a smooth surface, such as linoleum or a hardwood floor. This makes it easier to slide him into the correct "Down" position, even if he is reluctant to do it. Working on grass is also effective because it is smooth and softer for the dog to lie down on as opposed to a rough, hard sidewalk. Also, sidewalks become very hot and uncomfortable in the heat of the day.

The training should be given in the most positive area of your home or apartment, where your dog feels happiest and where he has never been aggressive. Use your good judgment about this. Train him wherever he feels good. For many dogs the best place is the kitchen or wherever he is fed. For others it is the yard, where he plays and has the most fun. If this is not possible, find a private place to train him, such as a quiet park with no distractions, no people, and no other dogs.

**The Paws Technique.** Before teaching a new command it is best to run through the commands the dog has been taught so that he begins on a positive note. With that accomplished you are ready to begin teaching the new command.

Place the dog in "Sit-Stay." Stand beside him as in "Heel." Hold the leash with the right hand. Leave a small amount of slack so it drapes across your knees. Pivot with your left foot and place your right foot in front of the dog.

**How to Obedience-Train an Aggressive Dog**

Bring both of your feet together once you face him. The leash should be held above the dog's head to keep him in position. Slowly kneel to the ground on one knee and take hold of both front paws just above his toes, with your free hand. Say the command "DOWWWWnnnn" and gently but firmly pull the front paws forward. When saying the command, extend the middle sound of the word so that it comes out in an exaggerated manner: "DOWWWWnnnn." Allow your voice to go down as you say the word. It helps the dog create an association with the action. He can learn what you expect from him by hearing the word go down in tone and drag on until his body is in the proper position.

Puppies, small dogs, and even-tempered dogs have no choice but to slide into the "Down" position when you pull their paws forward. Once the dog is in the "Down" position, praise him lavishly. Repeat this procedure at

least ten times and then give him a five-minute break. Allow him to pee but not to play. After the break, repeat the procedure until the dog offers no resistance to being pulled into the "Down" position. At this point please skip the other three techniques and go directly to "The Hand Signal," on page 150.

**The Foot Technique.** Have your dog perform all of the commands he has learned to this point and then begin to teach this technique.

Place the dog in "Sit-Stay." Stand beside the dog as in "Heel." Hold the leash with both hands. Allow a little more slack than usual so it drapes closer to the ground. Raise your left foot and place it on top of the leash at the center of the drape. Say, "DOWWWWnnnn." When saying the command, extend the middle sound of the

**How to Obedience-Train an Aggressive Dog**

word so that it comes out in an exaggerated manner: "DOWWWWnnnn." It helps the dog learn what you want when he hears the word go down in tone and drag on until his body actually lies in the proper position.

As your voice descends in tone, press the leash down with your left foot. This will force the dog to go down. Even a large, stubborn dog will have to move down if the floor is smooth. As you push down with your foot, you must slide the leash upward across the bottom of your shoe in the space between the heel and the sole. Do not pull up on the leash too quickly or in a harsh manner. As the dog moves to the ground, pull the leash up in a slow but steady manner. When the dog reaches the ground, praise him. Allow him to remain in the "Down" position for ten seconds and then say, "Sit." Praise him again and then say, "Stay," using the proper "Stay" hand signal as previously taught. Praise him again. Repeat this procedure at least ten times: "Down," praise. "Sit," praise. "Stay," praise. If the dog does not remain in "Stay" even after you correct him once or twice with a jerk of the leash, repeat the teaching procedures for "Stay" as described earlier in the chapter. If the dog has responded properly, take a five-minute break. Allow him to pee but not to play. After the break, repeat the procedures until the dog offers no resistance to going into the "Down" position. Please skip the other techniques and go directly to "The Hand Signal," on page 150.

**The Leg Technique.** It is important to practice each command the dog has learned before teaching this technique. This gets the dog to begin his new lesson with a positive feeling.

Begin. Place the dog in "Sit-Stay." Stand beside the dog as in "Heel." Hold the leash with the left hand. Face in the same direction as the dog. Slowly and gently kneel down next to your dog. Say, "DOWWWWnnnn." When saying the command, extend the middle sound of the word so that it comes out in an exaggerated manner: "DOWWWWnnnn." It helps the dog learn what you want when he hears the word go down in tone and drag on until his body actually lies in the proper position. As you firmly say the command word, place the dog in the "Down" position by lifting his right (or left) leg and pulling it forward. The leg you choose to lift depends on which one he favors. If he tends to place most of his weight on his right leg, then lift and pull his left leg. By lifting and pulling his leg forward, you give the dog no choice but to move into the "Down" position. The farther out you pull his leg, the less resistance he has to going down. Keep dragging out the command word

**How to Obedience-Train an Aggressive Dog**

"DOWWWWnnnn" until he has actually gotten into position on the ground and then praise him lavishly and enthusiastically. Repeat this at least ten times until he does not resist your action. He just might begin getting into the "Down" position without having to be pulled into it. Take a five-minute break. Allow the dog to pee but not to play. Please skip the next technique and go directly to "The Hand Signal," below.

**The Motivator Technique.** You can begin this lesson in a positive way by having your dog demonstrate how well he performs all the commands he has been taught up to this time. With that accomplished you may begin the new lesson.

This is the best technique to use for an aggressive dog or one that refuses to cooperate in the teaching process for any reason. The goal here is to gain the dog's confidence and entice him into working as well as for you to avoid

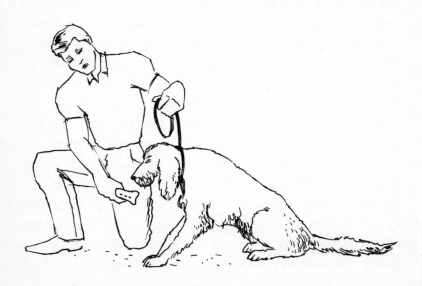

getting bitten. Select a motivator you think will work best, such as a food treat he really likes or one of the toys he enjoys. (*Do not use food as a motivator for a food-aggressive dog.*) The motivator of choice is used to capture the dog's interest, to keep him focused on the lesson, and to manipulate him into moving into the proper position for "Down."

Place the dog in "Sit-Stay." Stand next to him as in "Heel." Hold the leash with the left hand. Face in the same direction as the dog. Step a foot and a half in front of the dog, pivoting on your left foot as you did for the command "Sit-Stay." Remain standing. Hold the leash with the most comfortable hand, allowing about three feet of slack between you and the dog. Have the motivator in your other hand, ready to use as a lure.

Say, "DOWWWWnnnn." When saying the command, extend the middle sound of the word so that it comes out in an exaggerated manner: "DOWWWWnnnn." It helps the dog learn what you want when he hears the word go down in tone and drag on until his body actually lies in the proper position. As you firmly say the command word, hold the food or toy away from the dog's nose (from six inches for small dogs to twelve inches for large dogs). As you say the word "DOWWWWnnnn" and as your voice lowers on the "OWWWW," bring down your hand with the motivator in it all the way to the ground. If all goes well, the dog will follow it and inadvertently find himself in the "Down" position. Praise him immediately and give him the food or the toy. Raise the motivator once again above his head and say, "Sit!" Praise him if he obeys and correct him with a leash jerk if he does not. Then give him the command "Stay," using the proper hand signal. Give

**How to Obedience-Train an Aggressive Dog**

him the motivator each time he obeys the command along with lavish praise. Repeat the commands with the use of the motivators until the dog responds properly without the motivator: "Down," praise. "Sit," praise. "Stay," praise.

Take a five-minute break. Allow the dog to relieve himself but not to play. Go directly to "The Hand Signal," below.

**The Hand Signal.** The previous techniques taught the dog to go into the "Down" position on hearing the verbal command. This portion of the training teaches the dog to obey the command with a hand signal. This is extremely useful for commanding the dog from a distance to go "Down." Before going on to the next phase, run through the previous commands the dog has been taught so that he begins on a positive note and then move on to the hand signal.

Place the dog in "Sit-Stay." Kneel next to him, by his right side, facing in the same direction as the dog. Hold the leash with the right hand horizontally across your chest and keep it taut. Your left hand is free. Keep the leash tightly drawn so he cannot leave the position. Leave at least twelve inches of leash between his collar and your right hand. A playful dog may want to lick your face or jump on you. This is not permitted. A very aggressive dog may growl or snap. Either way, raise the leash so that he must go back to the "Sit" position after you say, "No! Good dog. Sit. Good dog. Stay. Good dog." Return the leash to a horizontal line across your chest. Flatten your left hand.

This is the most important part: Raise your left arm above the dog's head. Close your fingers together as if for a salute with your palm facing the ground. Say the command "DOWWWWnnnn" (extending the sound of the word as before) and lower your arm so that the dog can see it coming down, past his eyes and onto the top of the stretched-out leash, where it is clipped to the collar. It is essential that the leash be tight.

Because of the previous lesson, your dog should be lowering his body in response to the voice command. While you are still saying, "DOWWWWnnnn," your left hand should be in motion and touching the top of the leash, pressing it to the ground. It is important that your dog see this in his peripheral line of vision. Even though the dog is obeying the verbal command, he must be pushed to the ground by the force of your hand against the leash. Praise him with great enthusiasm when he gets into the "Down" position. Repeat this at least ten times.

The objective is to have your dog associate your lowering hand with the command "Down." If you do this properly your dog will always obey the "Down" command when he sees you lower your hand with your fingers flattened and your palm facing the ground. Once this is accomplished, you will be able to stand a good distance from the dog and simply give him the hand signal, to which he will respond as he should. If the dog does not respond properly or resists the teaching of this lesson, place him in "Sit-Stay" and begin again.

Once the dog is accustomed to seeing your hand come down onto the leash from the side, it is important to teach him to respond when your hand comes down from the front. Place him in "Sit-Stay" and stand next to him as in "Heel." Pivot around so that you are in front of him. Hold the leash with your left hand, keeping it taut, as before. Kneel on one knee, flatten your right hand, raise your right arm above your head, keeping it straight, and then say, "DOWWWWnnnn." As you say the command, you must lower your extended arm, in full sight of the dog, with the palm of your hand facing down, landing on top of the leash. Depending on the dog, you may or may not have to apply pressure to the leash to force him into the "Down" position. Praise the dog exuberantly once he reaches the ground. Repeat this procedure ten times or until the dog obeys both voice command and hand signal without experiencing the pressure of your hand.

One last step is necessary to complete the teaching of "Down." The dog must learn to respond to your voice command and your hand signal as you stand in front of him without applying pressure to the leash with your hand.

Stand two feet in front of your dog. Allow as much slack in the leash as possible and hold it with your left hand. Give him the command "Sit," and praise him for obeying. Next, give him the verbal command "Stay," using the hand signal as well, and again praise the dog for obeying. If he does not obey these commands, give him a leash correction while saying "No!" in a firm tone of voice. If he still does not obey, start over at the dog's side, as in "Heel." Repeat this procedure after making a pivotal turn to face the dog, as you have been doing.

If the dog has obeyed properly, you may continue the lesson. He should be in "Sit-Stay" while you stand two feet in front of him. Continue holding the leash with your left hand. Flatten your right hand as if for a salute with your palm facing the ground. Raise your right arm above your head in a straight vertical line. Say the command "DOWWWWnnnn" and lower your right arm onto the top of the leash at the same time. The dog will probably obey the command and go down without any pressure from the right hand. Praise him and start over again without moving from the frontal position. Give him the "Sit" and "Stay" commands, praising him each time, and then the "Down" command, repeating the above procedures ten times. Do not forget to give the hand signal and then offer enthusiastic praise.

Try repeating this procedure from greater distances. At first, give the commands from the end of the fully extended six-foot leash. If the dog continues to respond properly, use a fifteen- or thirty-foot training leash. At this point you may even try teaching the command without holding the leash at all. [*Do not try this unless you are indoors or within a fenced-off area.*] Be ready to step in quickly to grab the leash and correct him if he moves or bolts from the proper position.

If you are still experiencing success, try the command from two, three, or even six feet away without holding the leash, which should always be close by on the ground. Always be prepared to make a quick grab for the leash if the dog bolts. End the session by saying "Okay" in a happy, exuberant tone of voice. Allow the dog to pee and then walk him home.

### Down-Stay

**Performance:** The objective of this command is the same as "Sit-Stay," the difference being that the dog remains in a "Down" position. He is expected to remain in the "Down" position until you release him from it with another command or "Okay."

[*Note: If your dog growls or snaps at you whenever you try to touch him or approach him, cover his mouth with a soft nylon muzzle, as described in "Training Equipment," above. Use it before starting each lesson or until you feel safe. The muzzle will allow you to touch the dog and employ the teaching techniques without getting bitten.*]

Once your dog has learned "Sit-Stay," he should easily be able to adapt to "Down-Stay." The teaching technique is almost the same, with only minor differences. If necessary, refer to the "Sit-Stay" section earlier in this chapter.

After giving the command "Down" with the proper hand signal, give the dog his customary praise. Then say, "Stay," and use the appropriate hand signal (flattened hand placed several inches in front of the dog's eyes). Remove it quickly and once again praise the dog. Remember, he must be praised after executing each and every command. If the dog does not respond properly to "Down-Stay," repeat the teaching procedures of "Sit-Stay" but say the command "Down" instead of "Sit."

### Come When Called

**Performance:** The dog comes to you when you command him to do so and goes into a "Sit" position facing you and waits for your next command.

[*Note: If your dog growls or snaps at you whenever you try to touch him or approach him, cover his mouth with a soft nylon muzzle as described in "Training Equipment," above. Use it before starting each lesson or until you feel safe. The muzzle will allow you to touch the dog and employ the teaching techniques without getting bitten.*]

"Come When Called" is an important command, particularly when you need your dog to return to you for any reason at all, such as to avoid his running off or chasing someone. "Come When Called" involves a verbal command and a hand signal.

The command is best taught indoors but can be taught outdoors if the dog is confined in a fenced-off area. Allowing your dog to be off-leash and outdoors places his life in danger from auto traffic. Even the best-disciplined dogs have on occasion behaved impulsively when taken off-leash. But the command is very useful indoors and is well worth the teaching effort.

The basis of this command is making your dog ecstatic about running to you after being given the proper command. If you call him to you and then scold him, punish him, correct him, or make it unpleasant in any way, he is simply not going to obey the command "Come When Called." Why would he? Why would anyone return, only to be rejected or hurt in some way? It is important that your dog associate responding to your call with a gloriously happy experience. This command is about emotionally motivating your dog. If you must correct him and he is not close by, then you should *go to him* for that purpose. Never call him for a negative reason.

In commanding your dog to "Come When Called," always use the word "Okay," then his name, and then the command word "Come." It should be "Okay, Thunder, Come." The word "Okay" alerts your dog that you are about to give him a command, and that should get his attention. Say the word cheerfully so that he anticipates something pleasant. Using his name prepares him to move forward. The word "Come" tells him what to do. Be consistent about saying this command the same way each time. Make sure everyone in your family uses the command properly. Use only these precise words: "Okay, Thunder, Come." It is a dynamic command that will always serve you well once the dog learns to obey it. The command "Come When Called" has more often than not saved a dog's life.

An aggressive dog may challenge you by running in the opposite direction. Do not chase him, or he will continue to run. Do not show any anger or panic if he does this and do not threaten him. As hard as it may be, do not yell or get hysterical. Stay where you are and repeat the command as instructed: "Okay, Thunder, Come. Good boy." Never use his name negatively for any reason, because his name is an important part of this command and must always have a happy, pleasant association for him.

You cannot praise your dog enough for obeying the command. Lavish him with heaps of enthusiastic, joyful praise for every little thing connected with this command.

Your body language must never be threatening when teaching this command. Techniques that bring a dog to you, especially when he is challenging you, are bending down and enthusiastically calling him, clapping your hands pleasantly, and even running backward as you face him. Motivate your dog to come to you by using your body positively and in ways that get his attention.

Your voice should always be happy, enthusiastic, and loving. Your leash corrections should be a medium to firm jerk, but only when necessary and in keeping with the dog's size and age.

**The Technique.** When beginning this lesson, repeat everything the dog has learned up to now. Teach the new command by placing him in "Sit-Stay." With the leash in your left hand, stand in front of the dog, facing him, five feet away. Allow a slight slack in the leash. Bear in mind that the slightest pull of the leash will make him walk to you, which is not desirable without a verbal command.

Call the dog with the proper command, "Okay, Thunder, Come," in a very happy tone of voice. Make it sound like a wonderful occasion in order to motivate the dog to move forward and come to you. If he does, give him a lavish display of praise. It is highly likely that your dog will come to you on the first try. If he does, repeat the command at least ten times. If he does not come to you, then add more excitement to your voice. Almost any dog will respond. As a last resort, use as a motivator a small amount of food or a toy that you know the dog likes —

**How to Obedience-Train an Aggressive Dog**

**GRRR!**

but as a last resort only. If the dog jumps on you once he get to you, it is acceptable at this stage of the lesson.

Once again place the dog in "Sit-Stay." Stand in front of him, facing him, five feet away, with the leash in your left hand. Give him the command "Okay, Thunder, Come" while gently snapping the leash forward. The gentle snap of the leash should be on the word "Okay." When the dog moves to your feet, give him lots of praise. He should enjoy getting to you. In effect, he will have obeyed your command. Repeat this step at least ten times and take a break. Allow the dog to pee.

Next, teach the use of the hand signal. The hand signal for "Come When Called" is a simple one. Raise your right arm from the side of your body and swing it around and

**How to Obedience-Train an Aggressive Dog**

across your chest. It is the same gesture you would make to call someone from a distance. When you make this gesture you almost have to say, "Come here."

Place your dog in "Sit-Stay." Stand in front of him, facing him from five or six feet away, with the leash fully extended in your left hand. Give him the command "Okay, Thunder, Come" as you gently snap the leash forward, and then use the hand signal. Do not forget to snap the leash on the word "Okay." The dog should be praised lavishly when he gets to your feet. Repeat this procedure at least ten times. Take a five-minute break and then repeat the procedure ten more times.

The last part of the command is to get the dog to "Sit" once he gets to you after obeying the "Come When Called" command.

Place the dog in "Sit-Stay." Stand in front of the dog, facing him, five or six feet away, with the fully extended leash in your left hand. Give him the command "Okay, Thunder, Come," gently snapping the leash on the word "Okay." Give the hand signal, but as your arm moves forward, grab the leash and begin to pull it in, first with one hand and then with the other, so that it is eventually held over the dog's head tautly when he gets to your feet. If you hold the leash properly, the dog will have no choice but to go into a "Sit" position once he is directly in front of you. Give him the command "Sit," praise him lavishly, and then give him the command "Stay" accompanied by the proper hand signal, and once again praise him. Repeat this procedure at least ten times. End the session by saying "Okay," allow him to pee, and walk him home. Practice this command for six days but always start out by reviewing everything the dog has been taught in each preceding session.

### Place

**Performance:** At your command the dog stops whatever he is doing and leaves wherever he is doing it, walks to a designated place chosen by you (such as a corner of the room), and stays there after he is commanded to "Stay."

[*Note: If your dog growls or snaps at you whenever you try to touch him or approach him, cover his mouth with a soft nylon muzzle as described in "Training Equipment," above. Use it before starting each lesson or until you feel safe. The muzzle will allow you to touch the dog and employ the teaching techniques without getting bitten.*]

"Place" involves a verbal command and a hand signal. You must first decide where you want the dog's place to be located. It is most often on the floor in a corner of a room, such as the kitchen, living room, hallway, basement, or connecting garage. Before deciding, determine if you want the dog's place to be where he can see the family activities or not. You are advised not to make the dog's place in the same room where you dine because that gives him the opportunity to beg for food. It's a good idea to use a dog crate (with the door open at all times), a dog bed, a pillow, or a blanket to help establish the place and also to make it comfortable and inviting. Once you establish your dog's place you can now train him to go there on command. This often becomes the most used command in a busy household. Its usefulness is obvious.

All considerations for aggressive dogs as described in

the preceding lessons apply here as well. However, if your dog has been learning properly, he should not be a problem at this point. By now you should be able to determine how he will react to this or any other training situation and make the necessary adjustments that pertain to him.

Considering all that your dog has learned up to now, "Sit," "Sit-Stay," "Heel," "Automatic Sit," "Down," "Down-Stay," and "Come When Called," this command should be relatively easy to teach.

Start out by placing the training collar and six-foot leather leash on your dog while in the same room as the established *place*. Do this from the opposite side of the room from the established place.

Position yourself next to the dog's right side, facing in the same direction, as you would in the "Heel" position. Hold the leash taut in your left hand, about twelve inches above the dog's head. It is especially important that the verbal commands used in this lesson be given in an upbeat, cheerful, yet firm tone of voice.

Say "Bullet, Place!" Starting out with your left foot, walk the dog briskly to his place, turn around with him still at your side, and come to a full stop. Praise him for going there.

Next, give him the command "Sit" and praise him. Immediately afterward, say "Down," using the proper hand signal, and once again praise him. Say "Stay," using the hand signal. Praise him again, drop the leash, and walk to the other side of the room. If he tries to get up or leave the position, use a voice correction: "No!" If he goes back to his "Down" position, then praise him. If he does not, then repeat the "Down" and "Stay" commands, praising him after each one. If he holds the "Down-Stay" position for thirty seconds, call him to you, using the proper "Come When Called" command: "Okay, Bullet, Come." When he gets to you at the other side of the room and sits in front of you, heap tons of praise and compliments on him. Repeat this entire procedure from the beginning at least twenty times and take a five-minute break.

In the next session, repeat the procedure again but from another room. Give him the command "Bullet, Place!" Walk him to his place as before, holding the leash, say "Sit," and praise him. Say "Down," using the proper hand signal and praise him. Say "Stay," using the hand signal and praise him again. Drop the leash and walk to the room you started in. If he holds the "Down-Stay" position for thirty seconds, call him to you, using the proper "Come When Called" command: "Okay, Bullet, Come." When he gets to you in the other room and sits in front of you, heap tons of praise and compliments on him. Repeat this procedure twenty times and take a five-minute break.

From this point on, it is a matter of starting out the teaching procedure from other rooms and from greater distances. Start leaving the room after placing the dog in "Down-Stay" for longer periods of time. Go into the next room and extend the "Down-Stay" for one minute, two minutes, and so on. You know he has learned "Place" well when you can give him the command while you are both in another room and he leaves, goes straight to his established place, plops down, and stays there until you release him with the command "Okay" or "Okay, Bullet, Come."

Congratulations. Your aggressive dog is now obedience-trained and under a lot more control than ever before.

**How to Obedience-Train an Aggressive Dog**

Please bear in mind that obedience training for dogs requires constant practice and sharpening of both your delivery of the commands and the dog's performance of them. There is always more that a dog (and his owner) can learn. There are training classes you can attend or private training sessions from professionals. The more you train your aggressive dog, the more control you will have over him and the more you will be able to take him places. In that way you will be able to socialize your dog by getting him out and about in your community. This will make your dog a safer, more enjoyable companion, which is a better role for a dog. What every dog owner should want is a canine good citizen.

# 5

# Solving Your Dog's Aggressive-Behavior Problems

Dog owners living with an aggressive-behavior problem are usually agonized about what to do about it. The first phase for such owners is to deny that a problem exists and not even discuss the issue. Most people living out this nightmare make excuses for their dog's behavior, such as, "He only growls at strangers," or "There's something about that mailman that sets him off," or "He gets so jealous that he growls at anybody who comes near me," or "He only *nipped* the child. He didn't even break the skin."

How about this one? "Don't make sudden moves. Let him come to you and sniff. Don't look funny. When I tell him it's okay, slowly sit down. As long as I tell him you're okay, it will *be* okay. And for God's sake, don't get up too quickly or raise your voice. He may bite. Otherwise, the dog's a pussycat." How's that for a friendly, relaxed visit with a friend?

The sad thing is that all of these excuses will not solve an aggression problem, and the results can be devastating. People get bitten, lawsuits come under the door, everybody goes to court, and the possibility of having to give up a beloved dog is real.

Why do people feel the need to make excuses for their dog's aggressive-behavior problems? Possibly because they believe nothing can really be done about them, and the consequences are too painful to think about. In some cases it's a way of hiding from the unpleasant truth. They love their dogs and could never consider getting rid of them. But under the right circumstances, a court decision could force them to do just that. Some dog owners kid themselves into thinking the problem will go away on its own and that the dog will improve with age or that the problem isn't as bad as it seems. Another rationalization is that the dog's dangerous behavior makes him a good "watchdog." This way of thinking reflects avoidance of reality or a lack of knowledge about dog behavior, or both. If your dog has an aggressive-behavior problem, you will not be able to ignore it indefinitely. You owe it to yourself, your family, your community, and your dog to find out what can be done about it.

If you are serious about resolving a specific aggressive-behavior problem, you will find help in this chapter. However, you must first identify the dog's type of aggression, based on the tests and signs of aggression found in chapter 3, "How Aggressive *Is* Your Dog? Tests and Signs of Aggression." Second, you must obedience-train your dog with the complete course given in chapter 4, "How to Obedience-Train an Aggressive Dog."

If you want to resolve a behavior problem, we cannot

emphasize enough that obedience-training your dog is a major step toward finding the solution. Training your dog allows you to gain control over him and implement the proper correction procedures for dealing with aggressive behavior. The problem-solving techniques that this chapter offers are much more effective *after* your dog has been obedience-trained.

In addition to obedience-training your dog as an important step to solving any aggressive-behavior problem, there are two general approaches to all behavior problems that are of great importance. They are *socialization* and *desensitization*.

**Socialization.** Many aggressive dogs can benefit from this general approach to the problem. The idea is to reduce their aggressive behavior by exposing them to as many new people and situations as possible. By encouraging such dogs to interact with new people and places, you can create pleasant associations with them so that they eventually lose their fear and mistrust of them. Of course, it is not enough to have your dog interact with just your family. Your dog should learn to accept and eventually come to love your friends, your relatives, your friendly mailman, and all the people who visit you. An important part of socializing dogs is exposing them to many new and different environments and situations, including parks, busy streets, cars and traffic noises, crowds of people, and other dogs. They must learn how to be around joggers, skateboarders, cyclists, and other unfamiliar people and objects that move quickly.

People who live in rural or suburban areas tend to make the backyard their dog's home. The danger with doing this is that dogs living this way are likely to become unsocialized and territorially aggressive, which means they will become aggressive toward anyone and everyone they have never met and some they already know. A socialized dog living properly should be allowed to be both inside and outside his home, as a member of the family. He should be encouraged to sleep in the house. People who come to your home do not generally go to the backyard to visit your dog, and if that's where he is all the time, he will never have the opportunity to meet them and learn how to behave properly with them. An important aspect of socialization is having the entire family take part in raising and training their dog. A dog needs to be with all sorts of people and learn to love them to be a truly social dog.

**Desensitization.** By frequently exposing a dog to the people or situations that frighten, threaten, or challenge him, you can desensitize him to those things by creating pleasant associations with them. One of the ways to desensitize a frightened or aggressive dog is to socialize him, as described above. The more people and places the dog encounters, the more social he becomes. Desensitizing efforts should begin as soon as possible, no matter how young your dog. It is necessary to first recognize that your dog is fearful or aggressive and then become determined to change this behavior. Never try to justify aggressive behavior by thinking you have a great watchdog or that he's protecting your family, or by saying he dislikes only strangers. None of these ideas are valid.

Among the various reconditioning solutions that help desensitize your aggressive dog is the use of food treats. If he acts in a shy or aggressive manner with a stranger, that person should give him a food treat every time he or she comes in contact with the dog. This will create a pleasant association with that person and produce a positive response the next time the dog meets him or her. Eventually, he will become more trusting and less aggressive with most people. *If your dog is food-aggressive, do not use this technique.*

Another way to desensitize a dog is to use motivators, such as balls, toys, Frisbees, or anything that excites the dog or gives him pleasure. By introducing these motivators and having your dog associate them with new people, places, or situations, you will be able to recondition the dog with fewer aggressive responses and become better able to cope with his fear or aggressive behavior.

Some dogs suffer from phobias, such as the fear of noise. Desensitization is possibly the only effective technique available to cope with aggressive behavior stemming from phobias. For the fear of noise, a good technique to use for desensitization is an audiotape with various noises, such as thunder, a thunderstorm with a heavy downpour of rain, firecrackers, honking horns, gunshots, and various other noises that frighten the dog. These can be ordered from an accommodating music store. Start out by playing the specific noise that frightens your dog at a very low volume. Have your dog sit next to you and reassure him. Give him a lot of verbal and physical praise, a lot of "Good boy's," and even an occasional food treat as his reactions lessen in intensity. As his fear lessens, slowly increase the noise level in small increments until he eventually overcomes his phobia. You will be amazed how quickly he overcomes his fear.

## How to Use This Chapter

The techniques offered in this chapter attempt to solve specific aggressive problems through a reconditioning process, using corrections, distractions, and redirections each time your dog exhibits undesirable behavior. In many instances, the techniques are based on the same principle as obedience training, which is "praise and correction." Each behavior problem will be identified by where it occurs, such as in the kitchen, the backyard, the car, and so on. The solutions offered are based on the dog's age. One type or intensity of solution will be suggested for dogs less than one year of age, while other solutions will be suggested for dogs one year or older.

The following section, the Solutions Key, has ten separate techniques in it for solving your dog's behavior problems. Rather than repeating these techniques in each problem entry, we ask you to refer to the Solutions Key and read one or more of the ten techniques found there, identified by name and number. Some problems require several techniques from the Solutions Key and work together. You may want to try more than one technique for some problems if the first one does not work. Read through the Solutions Key at least once before searching for a specific problem entry.

### Solutions Key

1. *Changing the External Conditions that Create the Problem.* This technique addresses the problem of how the circumstances of the dog's day-to-day life can contribute to whatever the problem happens to be. In a way, we are talking about taking preventive measures. In most situations

the answer is simple and at times quite obvious. For example, an aggressive dog that is not confined and allowed to run loose is sooner or later going to get into trouble or make trouble. The preventive measure to be taken here is obvious. Confine the dog to one area and do not allow him to run loose. If he is not allowed to run around loose, he will not be able to chase cars, cyclists, rollerbladers, joggers, or anyone else. He cannot chase anyone or anything if you do not let him leave your property. If necessary, have a dog run made of chain-link fence fixed into a concrete slab or keep the dog in any fenced-in area. No dog should be allowed to run free, especially an aggressive one.

If your dog is aggressive about his possessions, do not

encourage this behavior with tug-of-war-type–games. Do not play games with an aggressive dog in which you pretend to hit him, grab him, wrestle with him, or goad him into barking or growling. If you do that, you are rewarding aggressive behavior and consequently teaching your dog to be aggressive.

Do not put your dog out of the house as a way of solving behavior problems such as house soiling or chewing. You will simply be trading one problem for another, which could turn out to be much worse. Some dogs become very aggressive once they are placed outdoors on their own and forced to cope with upsetting noises, passing strangers, other dogs, antagonizing children, and even well-meaning adults who do not recognize the difference between playing with a dog and taunting a dog. Work directly on solving the housebreaking or chewing problems from a book such as *When Good Dogs Do Bad Things* (Siegal and Margolis), and you will avoid the aggressive problems that develop outdoors.

If a dog suddenly and unexpectedly starts biting, it may be caused by pain from a medical problem of which you are not yet aware. Get him to a veterinarian for an examination.

Do not encourage your dog to scare people. If you do not want an aggressive dog, then do not reward aggressive behavior with praise, play, or treats. Do not allow your dog to become aggressive toward strangers who have legally entered your property and who are not a threat to you or anyone else. This includes letter carriers, delivery persons, utility workers, and so on.

Do not hit your dog in any way for any reason. Hitting a dog teaches him nothing except to fear you and then to defend himself with his teeth. Dog training does not require physical abuse or punishment. Control your frustration when the dog misbehaves and correct him as recommended in this Solutions Key. If your dog is shy, he should be brought under control with obedience training and then *socialized* by meeting as many new people and dogs as possible and brought into many different situations as well. Shy dogs can be socialized by lavishly rewarding and praising them for accepting other dogs, other people, and other places.

2. *Leash Correction.* This is the most important technique available for correcting a dog's aggressive behavior. Place the training collar around your dog's neck so that it forms the letter "P" and tightens and releases smoothly and efficiently. With the leash attached to the extended ring of the collar, gently test it for proper movement. It must tighten around the dog's neck when the leash is pulled and then loosen instantly when released. For more information about placing the leash and collar on the dog, see "How to Use the Training Collar and Leash" in chapter 4, "How to Obedience-Train an Aggressive Dog."

The leash correction consists of three elements. First, jerk the leash to the right, in a slightly upward direction, away from the right side of your body. The dog will experience a mild, negative sensation as the collar tightens around his neck. Next, as you jerk the leash, say "No!" in a firm tone of voice. This is a verbal correction, and it will communicate to the dog that he has not performed properly. The jerking motion of the leash should not be so hard as to knock the dog off his feet. However, it should be firm enough to tighten the training collar, creating a mild, negative sensation. The snapping sound of the metal links has as much corrective value as the tightening of the collar. For this reason there is no need to jerk the leash hard, except for the largest, most stubborn dogs. Finally, immediately after jerking the leash, you must generously praise the dog in a happy, friendly tone of voice, almost thanking him for responding well to your correction, even if he didn't.

Practice the snapping motion of the correction by placing the training collar around your left wrist and pretending it is the dog's neck. Do everything as previously described so that you get a sense of how hard to pull the leash in a correction without hurting the dog. Do not become overzealous. Never correct your dog unless it is necessary. Too many corrections will ruin the effectiveness of the technique and make him apprehensive every time you bring out the leash.

Not every dog is the same. When administering a leash correction, you must consider each dog individually in terms of his age, size, sensitivity, temperament, and degree of aggressiveness. Common sense should dictate how firm or how soft to make your corrections. You should not give a dog a leash correction while you are teaching him the basics of a command. However, once he has demonstrated that he has learned the command, it is fair to correct him if he refuses to obey or makes a mistake. In dog training, he must respond on command. If he does not respond properly, the dog owner should administer a reminder using the leash correction. This is negative reinforcement. The praise that comes immediately afterward is positive reinforcement.

To review the leash correction: Jerk the leash quickly and firmly *to the right,* in an *upward* direction, whenever the dog behaves aggressively, refuses to obey, or makes a mistake. As you do this, say "No!" in a firm tone of voice. Release the tension on the leash instantly and then praise the dog lovingly. That is a proper leash correction.

3. *Verbal Correction.* A verbal correction is simply the word "no" spoken in a firm, no-nonsense tone of voice. The verbal correction can be part of a leash correction or used in conjunction with a shake can, a spray bottle, or by itself. Do not underestimate the effectiveness of a sharp verbal correction once the dog's behavior has been modified with leash corrections. However, once your dog responds properly to leash corrections that include verbal corrections, he will give you the same obedient response to the verbal correction alone without the use of the leash. The verbal correction is as important and precise a training and reconditioning tool as anything you will ever use if it is done properly.

The verbal correction is most effective when you say "No!" clearly and in a tone of voice that indicates you are in charge. Use your voice in a way that sounds natural and familiar to the dog but with the distinction that you are not playing around and that you are not intimidated by his aggressive behavior. See "Getting Your Dog's Attention with 'No' and 'Okay,'" in chapter 4, "How to Obedience-Train an Aggressive Dog."

To administer a verbal correction, say "No!" in a firm tone of voice. As the dog begins to respond properly, praise him, but measure how enthusiastic you should be with him. If you become too enthusiastic and if the dog is off-leash, he will run up to you to be petted, and that may or may not be appropriate depending on the situation and what your objective is at that moment. That said, it is better to misjudge with too much praise rather than not enough.

4. *Muzzle.* The soft nylon muzzle can be an important tool for implementing all of the solutions for aggressive problems in this key. Use this effective piece of equipment in situations where the dog growls, threatens you, or attempts to bite. This is especially useful when a dog is possessive-aggressive over toys, food, or territory. By using the muzzle you will be able to handle the dog safely as you execute corrections and other solution techniques. You will be able to work with the dog in close quarters for specific problems as well as obedience training, especially with the "Down" command. In these situations you will not have to worry about getting bitten. It is a fact that many aggressive problems become reduced or fade away entirely once a dog has been obedience-trained. (See "Training Equipment" in chapter 4, "How to Obedience-Train an Aggressive Dog.")

5. *Wire Dog Crate.* Although the dog crate is most useful for housebreaking and keeping a dog out of trouble, it can also be used as a safety tool when addressing aggressive-behavior problems. For example, if your dog is aggressive over food, toys, or other aspects of territory, place him in the crate before exposing him to those things. In that way you can never get bitten. If he growls or snaps at you as you handle the sensitive objects, you must distract him or correct him as a way of changing his behavior.

You can recondition a dog that is confined in a wire crate by distracting or correcting him with a shake can or spray bottle when he growls or snaps. Do not forget to praise the dog after giving him a correction. The same is true of leash corrections or verbal corrections. To administer a leash correction with the dog in the crate, attach the leash to his collar, run it through the wire openings of the crate, and then jerk the leash when it is appropriate. Place the dog's food outside the crate but next to him. Go near the food, touch it, walk around him, and touch his bowl again. If he shows any aggression, give him a leash correction, say "No!," praise him, and give him a food treat. In extreme cases use a muzzle and try feeding the dog outside the crate. Always be upbeat and enthusiastic with your dog when placing him in the crate and when relating to him once he is inside. Do nothing that allows him to associate the crate with punishment. Praise him enthusiastically for every little thing.

It is important to use a wire dog crate so that you can apply the recommended methods through the wire openings as the dog looks out at you. If he can see what's going on around him he will not be too upset about being in the crate. The main point to confining an aggressive dog in a wire crate is to avoid getting injured as you apply the reconditioning techniques suggested here. You can also watch the dog's reactions to your reconditioning procedures and gauge his progress. At times the dog will be very aggressive in the crate but that will change as you become more in control and he accepts that fact. In any event, you will always be safe.

6. *Use of Food.* Although using food for training an even-tempered dog is never recommended, it is a useful method when trying to cope with a severe aggression problem or for defusing a dangerous situation. The use of food is effective when used sparingly as a reward for good conduct. Food treats help create a bond with very aggressive dogs, which in turn initiates the acceptance of obedi-

ence training. For example, food can be used as a lure if a dog has grabbed something and takes refuge under a table or chair and growls or otherwise threatens you when you approach him. Offer him his favorite food treat in order to get him to come out without biting you. If the dog has been obedience-trained, use the command "Come When Called" in a very friendly voice and offer him the food. When the dog obeys the command, praise him as you give him the food.

When using food as a lure it is possible to interrupt the dog's sequence of behavior that leads to a bite. If you use the dog's favorite food you might stop his aggressive behavior for the time being and get him to come toward you and the food. In a risky situation you must do whatever is possible.

7. *Shake Can*. The shake can is another correction or distraction tool. As explained in "Correction Tools" in chapter 4, "How to Obedience-Train an Agressive Dog," it is simply a clean, empty soda or juice can with ten pennies inside, sealed closed with tape. It is meant to create a loud, distracting sound when shaken. It must always be accompanied with a verbal correction. When the dog is in the act of misbehaving, shake the can vigorously and say "No!" in a loud, firm tone of voice. Praise the dog generously immediately following the correction. If you place a number of these inexpensive, easy-to-make corrective tools in strategic places in your home, you will be able to correct the dog no matter where he is or what he is doing, even if he is not on-leash.

8. *Spray Bottle Filled with Water*. This reconditioning tool is used to stop a dog's aggressive behavior by distracting or correcting him. Squirt water in his face from the

spray bottle whenever he growls or snaps at you. It is meant to stop his aggressive action. This is useful whether the dog is on- or off-leash. Squirt water at the dog and say "No!" in a firm tone of voice. Praise him generously immediately afterward. If the dog continues to threaten you, start using the soft muzzle right away.

9. *Garden Hose.* This common household utensil can be used outdoors to stop serious aggressive situations. Hose the dog with water in order to stop a dogfight, chasing of a passerby, or the frenzied fighting between two dogs on opposite sides of the same fence. Use the garden hose for *any* aggressive behavior that requires strong action.

10. *Doorbell.* This technique should not be used if your dog becomes agitated or aggressive at the sound of the doorbell. Ringing the doorbell is useful for alleviating tension and as a way of distracting a dog away from his aggressive behavior. If he is under the table growling for food, for example, it can be dangerous to try to remove him by pulling him out with your hands. Ringing the doorbell is very likely to divert his attention and get him to drop what he's doing and leave the table to see what's going on. As the bell rings, call him to you in a happy, upbeat tone of voice. If he comes to you, lavish him with praise. If he is obedience-trained, use the command "Come When Called," never failing to praise the dog when he responds properly. Although it may not work every time, it is worth trying. If he responds predictably, the ringing doorbell will disrupt his aggressive responses and relieve pressure from the situation, thus avoiding a biting incident. Once he is out from under the table, place a leash and training collar on him so he can be corrected if necessary. *Do not give the dog a leash correction immedi-*

*ately after he has come to you or he may never come to you again.* This is a good example of changing external conditions in order to stop the continuation of aggressive behavior.

### Aggressive-Behavior Problems

Here are the most frequently seen aggressive-behavior problems and where they occur. The problems are plainly described, and solutions are suggested for both dogs less than one year of age and those one year of age or older. When it is indicated, please look for the suggested solutions as they are numbered in the Solutions Key, above.

## The Kitchen or Dining Room

**Problem:** Your dog growls or snaps at you when you try to take his food away, walk by his food, or touch him while he's eating. Any form of aggressive behavior involving his food should be considered a problem that needs to be addressed.

**Solutions:** If your dog is less than one year of age, go to the Solutions Key and utilize the Leash Correction (2), Spray Bottle Filled with Water (8), or Shake Can (7) solutions. Hand-feeding is worth trying if your dog is not a biter. Allow him to eat some of his meal directly out of your open palm in order to get him to accept humans touching his food. If your dog is over one year of age, use Leash Correction (2), Muzzle (4), or Wire Dog Crate (5).

**Problem:** Your dog steals food. When you try to take it away from him, he runs and hides. If you then try to take it from him, he reacts aggressively.

**Solutions:** Bear in mind that the problem addressed here is the dog's aggressive behavior, not his stealing food. For dogs of any age, go to the Solutions Key and try the Doorbell (10), calling him to you after the ringing distracts him. Another method for getting him out of hiding without your getting bitten is to use a ball or a toy as a way of motivating him to leave the room and follow you. Praise him generously when he does. You can prevent the problem in the first place by not leaving any food out on kitchen counters or tables where the dog can get it. It is important whenever possible to avoid situations that provoke aggressive behavior.

**Problem:** Your dog is under the kitchen table and he growls at you when you try to pick up food that has dropped to the floor. When children are at the table, quite a bit of food is likely to fall to the floor, and the dog's aggressive response will be repeated often.

**Solutions:** For dogs of any age, prevention is the most important solution to this problem. Do not allow the dog to be in the kitchen or dining room when you or your family is eating. Remove him whenever you are preparing food or are about to have a meal. Teach your dog the obedience commands "Down," "Down-Stay," and "Place," as described in chapter 4, "How To Obedience-Train an Aggressive Dog." These commands are particularly useful when you are faced with this problem.

**Problem:** The dog goes into the garbage container to steal food, and when you try to take it from him or shoo him away, he growls or tries to bite. This problem may occur with uneaten food or with such inedible items as bones, eggshells, coffee grounds, and all the rest.

**Solutions:** Go to the Solutions Key for dogs of any age and try the Doorbell (10) technique. After the doorbell has rung, call the dog to you in a happy, enthusiastic tone of voice. Use motivators such as a ball or a toy to lure him away from the garbage. Your extremely enthusiastic tone of voice will get the dog to follow you out of the room. Keep praising him lavishly as he moves toward you. You can prevent this aggressive-behavior response by keeping a tight lid on your garbage container or by using a bitter repellent on it. Bitter Apple is a commercial product created for this purpose, or you may simply make a paste of water and alum (obtained at a pharmacy).

**Problem:** You live with two dogs and they behave aggressively when you feed them.

**Solutions:** For dogs of any age, this problem will rear its ugly head when you feed them at the same time or in the same room. When you do that, you create the conditions for aggressive behavior about competition for territory, possessions, and the order of social rank. Obviously, the answer lies in not feeding the dogs together. Moreover, they should be fed in different parts of your house. Never give both of your dogs treats or snacks when they are together, and this applies to dogs of any age.

**Problem:** Your dog becomes aggressive when you feed him from your table. He may also behave aggressively when you use food as part of a game, such as offering it to him and withdrawing it before he can get it. Such games are a form of teasing the dog with his food. He may eventually bite you as he looks for the food. After all, where is the food? It is in your hand, and that's what he's going to bite.

**Solutions:** No matter what the dog's age, puppy or old-timer, you must use your common sense here. Do not offer food from the table or anywhere else but in his own bowl. And never tease your dog, especially an aggressive dog, with food or snacks.

**The consequences of these problems.** If there are children in your home their natural curiosity will tempt them to approach the dog as he eats. If they go near a food-aggressive dog while he is eating, they are quite likely to get growled at or even bitten, depending on the dog. It could be disastrous. Visitors not familiar with the dog's behavior are also in danger. That could lead to serious injuries, hospital bills, lawsuits, and even court orders to dispose of the dog.

If the dog is ever sick and you have to take something from his mouth or medicate him, you will be putting yourself in jeopardy if he is food-aggressive. Dealing with food-aggressive dogs presents many different, serious problems.

A food-aggressive dog, whether he is a puppy or an adult, should be trained before someone gets hurt. Even a small dog in the six-pound range can be dangerous if he is extremely aggressive. Of course, large dogs have a greater potential for injury than others do. Imagine a full-grown Rottweiler, German Shepherd Dog, or Golden Retriever that goes for you when you approach his food bowl.

**Why is this happening?** The cause of aggressive responses in the above situations could represent one category of aggression or a combination of categories, such as possessive aggression (protecting his food), territorial aggression (protecting his space), and, possibly, fear aggression (protecting himself).

This behavior may have started when the dog was a puppy. If he was part of a large litter, where there were more puppies than nipples, he may have had to struggle or fight for milk from his mother's breast. This can create a special response to anyone coming near his food.

In some situations puppies that have been weaned to solid food are fed in one large, communal bowl. A puppy that was bullied or one that did the bullying at the bowl will likely become a food-aggressive dog. In some situations one puppy is bullied by all of his littermates because he is the runt of the litter. Such a puppy can grow into a fear-aggressive dog, particularly about his food.

Perhaps the dog was a stray and had to fend for himself on the street. To survive he would have had to search garbage cans or anyplace else where he might find food. As far as the dog is concerned, every meal could have been his last, so he learned to protect it as if his life depended on it, which it may have.

Food-aggressive behavior will certainly develop when there are two dogs in the home and one keeps stealing the other's food. The dog that goes hungry is not only going to get aggressive with the other dog, but he may also behave the same way with humans who approach his food.

If your dog behaves aggressively over food and you believe this is acceptable or that the dog is probably right to respond with aggression, then you are a large part of the problem. It is common for some people to believe that if it were their food, they wouldn't want somebody bothering it, either. The truth is that when you allow food aggression to continue unchecked, you are opening the door to all kinds of aggressive behavior. One kind of aggressive behavior can lead to other kinds in a variety of situations.

Domesticated dogs must behave appropriately for the human setting. In the wild, aggressive behavior is necessary. A dog living as part of a pack quite naturally protects his food if another pack member goes for it. Unless you have established in your dog's mind that you are the leader of his pack and are dominant, he will assume that role and exhibit aggressive behavior. This kind of behavior must not be allowed in a home environment. It is unacceptable and dangerous.

## The Bedroom, Family Room, or Any Other Room with Furniture

**Problem:** The dog is on the bed or furniture and growls or bites when you try to move him off, especially if he is asleep. He may also become aggressive if you try to wake him or even go near him. In some cases it happens just because you entered the room.

**Solutions:** No matter what age your dog is, teach him the obedience commands "Come When Called" and "Place." See chapter 4, "How to Obedience-Train an Aggressive Dog."

For dogs less than one year of age, go to the Solutions Key and read Changing the External Conditions that Create the Problem (1). You can prevent this behavior if you do not allow the dog on the bed or furniture at any time or under any conditions, including not having him on

your lap as you sit or lie down. Prevention is the best so-lution. Also in the Solutions Key, employ Leash Correc-tion (2), Doorbell (10), Verbal Correction (3), and Shake Can (7). If your dog is over one year of age, read Changing the External Conditions That Create the Problem (1) in the Solutions Key and keep your dog off the bed or furni-ture. In addition, try Leash Correction (2), Muzzle (4), and Verbal Correction (3).

**The consequences of this problem.** If this behav-ior is allowed to continue, you will have a dog that is ag-gressive most of the time and in all situations that displease him. In effect your dog will be running the house. Eventually, a territorial-aggressive dog is going to bite someone he feels is invading his territory, and that could be anyone, including those in his family.

If a child visits your home and he or she gets on the

bed or couch, how will your territorial-aggressive dog react? The problem is especially dangerous if no children live with you and your dog is not used to the impulsive behavior of youngsters. Dogs are not fair in human terms. Territorial aggression is not limited to the bed or the furniture. This aggression can transfer to any part of the house or to any person.

If these issues are not addressed and this behavior is not changed, you may be forced to find another home for the dog.

**Why is this happening?** Dogs have an instinct to create a den, and in our homes many things can substitute for this. The den can be the floor, a dog crate, a bed, or a soft piece of furniture. Once a dog that is very territorial has claimed an area to be his exclusive den, he protects it from anyone, including his family.

Some people sleep with their dogs, especially if they are puppies or very small. Within one or two years, such dogs can become possessive about the person with whom they are sleeping. A shy or fear-ridden dog will not only become strongly attached to that person but abnormally protective as well. The closer anybody gets, the more aggressive the dog becomes.

### Front Door

**Problem:** Your dog becomes aggressive when a stranger, neighbor, or delivery person approaches the front door or is invited in. If your dog barks and backs away or remains very close to your side and then chases the visitor as he begins to leave, it is a major problem with a dangerous potential.

**Solutions:** For dogs of any age, teach the commands

"Sit", "Down," "Down-Stay," and "Place." See chapter 4, "How to Obedience-Train an Aggressive Dog."

For dogs less than one year of age, go to the Solutions Key and apply Changing the External Conditions That Create the Problem (1), Leash Correction (2), Verbal Correction (3), Muzzle (4), Use of Food (6), and Shake Can (7).

For dogs over one year of age, go to the Solutions Key and apply Changing the External Conditions That Create the Problem (1), Leash Correction (2), Verbal Correction (3), Muzzle (4), Doorbell (9), and Shake Can (7).

**The consequences of this problem.** Your dog may bite someone because he thinks he is protecting you or his territory. If he does, you will have to pay for that person's medical expenses and hope you are not taken to court.

**Why is this happening?** You send a mixed message to your dog when you tell him, "It's okay," as he stands by your side and barks or growls and shows other signs of active aggression to the visitor at your door. You think you are calming him down and getting him to stop, but the dog accepts your soothing tone as a reward for his behavior. You should be correcting him instead of saying his name along with nicely worded pleas for him stop.

Visitors trying to act unafraid do not usually fool dogs that are behaving aggressively. Most dogs can read negative body language exceptionally well and take advantage of this by continuing their threatening behavior.

A dog may become startled by the sudden movement of a visitor coming through the front door and back away or react in any number of aggressive ways, such as chasing that person.

If your dog is by your side and becomes aggressive as someone reaches out to you (he may actually bite or lunge at that person), it is because of an intense sense of territory about his home and those in it. This is an aspect of pack behavior, even though it is inappropriate for a human situation. It could mean that your dog has become too dominant within his pack because he was never corrected properly for this behavior.

When a letter carrier or delivery person comes to your home at about the same time every day, the dog that barks or growls at him is convinced that he's making that person leave. Dogs are born with an instinct to hunt and chase prey animals or invaders. When the person a dog barks or growls at leaves the property, the dog feels dominant. As time passes, such a dog will become more aggressive and more territorial toward anyone or anything entering his territory.

## Front and Backyards

**Problem:** A dog that is allowed to be loose becomes aggressive and too protective when encountering visitors, delivery people, and others lawfully entering your property. Of course, no one should allow a dog to run loose when there is a leash law in force.

**Solutions:** For dogs of all ages teach the commands "Down," "Down-Stay," and "Place." See chapter 4, "How to Obedience-Train an Aggressive Dog."

For dogs less than one year of age refer to the Solutions Key and use Changing the External Conditions That Create the Problem (1), Leash Correction (2), Verbal Correction (3), Shake Can (7), and Garden Hose (9).

For dogs over one year of age, refer to the Solutions Key

and use Changing the External Conditions That Create the Problem (1), Leash Correction (2), Verbal Correction (3), Muzzle (4), Shake Can (7), and Garden Hose (9).

**Problem:** A dog may behave aggressively when tied up. This should be viewed as a warning that he may bite in order to protect his space.

**Solution:** Do not tie up or chain down your dog. Ideally, he should be behind an enclosed chain-link dog run. You must find a way to confine your dog without forcing him to be in one tiny location, as imposed by a rope or a chain.

**Problem:** Your dog chases joggers, cyclists, or anyone else moving quickly past his front or backyard. If he is confined to his area, he will frantically run back and forth along the fence as he barks and growls. Should he get loose, he will chase his prey until they leave what he considers his territory. If this behavior goes uncorrected, the dog will eventually attack and bite someone.

**Solutions:** For dogs of all ages, teach the commands "Down," "Down-Stay," "Place," and "Come When Called." See chapter 4, "How to Obedience-Train an Aggressive Dog."

For dogs less than one year of age, refer to the Solutions Key and use Changing the External Conditions That Create the Problem (1), Leash Correction (2), Verbal Correction (3), Shake Can (7), and Spray Bottle Filled with Water (8).

For dogs over one year of age, refer to the Solutions Key and use Changing the External Conditions That Create the Problem (1), Leash Correction (2), Verbal Correction (3), Muzzle (4), Shake Can (7), and Garden Hose (9).

**Problem:** A dog may become aggressive if he's sleeping under the porch or behind a bush and someone enters the yard. If he suddenly wakes up and notices a stranger invading his territory, he will defend it.

**Solutions:** For dogs of any age, go to the Solutions Key and read Changing the External Conditions That Create the Problem (1), Wire Dog Crate (5), Verbal Correction (3), Shake Can (7), and Garden Hose (9). You may try to desensitize your dog to strangers. Read "Desensitization" and "Socialization" at the beginning of this chapter.

**Problem:** Your dog unexplainably becomes aggressive toward a service person, such as a pool cleaner or gardener who enters the premises on a regular basis. This may come as a surprise, since the dog has met the person a number of times before without incident. Dog owners are always shocked when their dog bites someone because they never recognize the signs.

**Solutions:** For dogs of any age, go to the Solutions Key and read Changing the External Conditions That Create the Problem (1), Wire Dog Crate (5), Verbal Correction (3), Shake Can (7), and Garden Hose (9).

**Problem:** The dog growls, snaps, nips, and perhaps bites when his owners allow him to run around the house loose during a party or at an outdoor barbecue. The aggression may come when the guests give the dog food treats. Bending over the dog, even kissing him may be considered an invasion of his territory by some aggressive dogs. Dogs who love their families may not feel the same toward anybody else.

**Solutions:** For dogs of any age, go to the Solutions Key and read Changing the External Conditions That Create the Problem (1) and Wire Dog Crate (5).

**The consequences of these problems.** The situations above are prime examples of territorial aggression. The dog's aggressive behavior is based on his need to protect his home. It goes to his natural instinct to keep his den free from potentially harmful strangers. Dogs become dangerous when their owners fail to recognize the signs of aggression such as overprotectiveness, growling, or nipping fingers. Add to that the lack of obedience training or behavior modification of any kind and you have a lawsuit in your future. Imagine a dog getting out, seeing a child running down the street, and biting the child because the dog has been kept in his yard his whole life.

If a dog spends too much time alone in the yard or is always tied up, he will not become socialized and therefore will not be capable of adapting to new people or different environments. A dog like that is usually uncontrollable and far too aggressive to be trusted or enjoyed as a companion. These are problems created by dogs *and* the people responsible for them.

It's a *dog problem* because dogs protect themselves and survive by using their natural territorial instincts. It's a *people problem* because we want dogs to protect us from bad people, but how does a dog distinguish a good guy from a bad guy? The truth is he cannot.

**Why does this happen?** Unless a dog is trained to be a social animal, which means he can interact with everybody, his owners create the problem. If your dog is shy or continually frightened as he grows into an adult, and if he's not comfortable with unfamiliar people, he will become bolder as he matures and aggressive with anyone invading his space. He may eventually become a biter. Some dogs become aggressive because their owners encourage it.

## Two Dogs in the Same House

**Problem:** More than one dog lives in the same home, and they constantly fight with each other. Even two dogs that grew up together as puppies will fight over food, territory, owner attention, or sleeping areas as they reach maturity. Dogs may behave well when alone in the house but become aggressive when the owners are home and involved with either one of the dogs.

**Solutions:** Aggressive behavior usually occurs between two males or two females. Prevention is the most effective solution. The most important preventive measures for this problem are acquiring dogs of the opposite sex only and then having them surgically neutered. If you are thinking about adding another dog to your household, make sure it's of the opposite sex. Of course, if you live with three or more dogs, gender selection offers no solution. In this situation you must pay more attention to the most dominant of the dogs and allow him to be top dog. They will create an order of rank among themselves. It is absolutely imperative to obedience-train the dogs so that you can maintain control over their behavior if and when they fight. Give them separate toys, food bowls, and other possessions to avoid things to fight about. With three or more dogs, the command "Place" is extremely valuable. See chapter 4, "How to Obedience-Train an Aggressive Dog."

If it is too late and you already live with two males or two females, your options are limited. The main course of action is to keep them separated as much as possible. Two dogs in the same house should be fed and watered in different rooms, in different bowls. Give them each their own place to sleep, on separate dog beds or in separate dog crates. Do not walk the dogs together. Never give them food treats or toys at the same time. Do this on a one-at-a-time, individual basis. The worst thing is giving two male dogs bones at the same time. They will fight over them. Play with the dogs separately.

The most important thing you can do is obedience-train both dogs. See chapter 4, "How To Obedience-Train an Aggressive Dog." Go to the Solutions Key and read all ten solutions. Use any or all of them where they seem appropriate.

**The consequences of this problem.** If you interfere with two same-sex dogs in the same house as they fight, you or somebody else may get bitten, especially if they are fighting over those things that matter most to them, such as food, possessions, territory, or sleeping space. In a fight between the two, the dogs are more likely to bite each other, which could result in stitches, infection, lost coat, and scars.

If there is no peace between the two dogs, you might be forced to give up one of them. This happens frequently when two people meet and they each own a dog of the same sex. To prevent violent aggressive episodes, you must set up rules for managing the dogs properly. This is important for the sake of the relationship of the humans as well as the dogs.

If you acquire two dogs of the same sex as puppies and they grow up together, they grow up in a sort of mini-pack and fight for dominance in all things pertaining to them, including their owners' attention. They will look cute as puppies while they're fighting. As they mature, their fights will become less cute and more frightening, especially if both dogs are dominant. If you have two dominant dogs, the issues become serious and their fights become increasingly violent. A dominant and a subordinate dog, even of the same sex, live fairly well together once they establish the social order of rank.

**Why does this happen?** When two same-sex dogs living in the same house constantly fight, it is usually based on a combination of dominant aggression and territorial aggression in addition to their need to protect as well as possess the owner or various members of the family. The heart of the problem is the question of who is leader of the dog pack. A dominant and subordinate dog usually work things out if you allow the dominant one to be top dog. It is a mistake to favor the subordinate dog. That will only make the dominant dog aggressive and cause him to attack the subordinate dog. Sometimes the problem is provoked when both dogs are allowed on the same bed, or when the dog who got there first is the only one allowed up. In those circumstances a fight could ensue if one of the dogs simply enters the room. Feeding the dogs together, keeping the dogs together most of the time, and encouraging them to compete over anything at all promotes this form of aggressive behavior.

Some well-intentioned people acquire a second dog as a companion for their first dog only to discover that they have created a long-term, never-ending dogfight. If the new dog was adopted he might have been abused by other dogs or people, or could have been the abuser himself of other dogs. He may never have been socialized with other dogs. Dogs that have had good experiences with other dogs do not automatically pick dogfights. If you have no knowledge of your new dog's history, anything can happen. Your best opportunity to prevent a dogfight relationship is to make sure you keep dogs of the opposite sex and to learn as much as possible about your new dog's history and behavior *before you accept him.*

### Walking Outside with the Dog On-Leash

**Problem:** Your dog begins growling, snarling, and pulling on the leash to confront another dog of the same sex.

**Solutions:** Dogs of any age with this problem must be obedience-trained and learn to obey all the commands taught in chapter 4, "How To Obedience-Train an Aggressive Dog." The dog owner must have total control over his or her dog with this problem. Go to the Solutions Key and read Changing the External Conditions That Create the Problem (1), Leash Correction (2), Verbal Correction (3), and Muzzle (4).

**Problem:** Your dog reacts aggressively when a stranger approaches and in a friendly manner sticks out his hand.

**Solutions:** If a territorial-aggressive dog has ever been hit he will react negatively toward anyone extending their hands to him for any reason. Based on the dog's experience, the gesture appears to be a threat. For dogs less than one year of age, go to the Solutions Key and read Changing the External Conditions That Create the Problem (1), Leash Correction (2), and Verbal Correction (3). For dogs over one year of age go to the Solutions Key and read Muzzle (4).

**Problem:** Your dog becomes aggressive and lunges at joggers, skateboarders, cyclists, or people on rollerblades who come too close to him and move with quick, jerky motions.

**Solutions:** This is a classic example of territorial behavior. The dog becomes aggressive because of his possessiveness over the space he occupies and the owner at his side. If your dog is obedience-trained, utilize the commands "Heel," "Sit," "Down," and "Down-Stay" when the problem arises. If he isn't, it is important that you train him. See chapter 4, "How to Obedience-Train an Aggressive Dog." If your dog is less than one year of age, go to the Solutions Key and read Changing the External Conditions That Create the Problem (1), Leash Correction (2), and Verbal Correction (3). If your dog is over one year of age, go to the Solutions Key and utilize Muzzle (4).

**The consequences of these problems.** Your dog may injure someone who is enjoying a legitimate outdoor activity. When he lunges, he may possibly nip or bite someone even if he is on a leash. If he manages to break loose from the leash he will be capable of attacking someone and thus becomes a dangerous menace. If this problem is not corrected, there is always the strong possibility of a major lawsuit involving a loss of money and a court order to isolate the dog, which only makes his behavior problem worse.

**Why does this happen?** This behavior is a serious problem because it is based on the dog's territorial temperament, which can be brought under control but not changed. A territorial-aggressive dog feels compelled to protect his space. It is the owner's problem because he or she must learn to recognize the signs of this form of aggression, such as his body language, his posture, or his stare, and then take the proper precautions. See chapter 3, "How Aggressive *Is* Your Dog? Tests and Signs of Aggression." The owner of such a dog must watch for the signs of aggression, and when he or she sees them, correct the dog appropriately.

The conflict between protection and aggression is difficult for dog owners to grasp. They seem to want a dog that will protect them but fail to understand that the price for this is usually uncontrolled, indiscriminate, aggressive behavior toward anyone who violates the dog's space.

### In the Car

**Problem:** Your dog is locked inside the car and growls, snarls, barks, bites, or lunges toward the window or retreats into a corner of the backseat as strangers approach. When someone other than you reaches for him, he becomes aggressive. He may behave this way if an unknown person merely gets near the car.

**Solutions:** For dogs of any age, go to the Solutions Key and read Changing the External Conditions That Create the Problem (1), Verbal Correction (3), Shake Can (7), and Spray Bottle Filled with Water (8). An important option for avoiding injuries is to confine the dog in a wire dog crate, strapped down to the back of the car with the seat belt. There are dog crates designed to use inside a car.

**The consequences of these problems:** There is no way to know what your dog's reaction is going to be when strangers approach your car and you're not there. The dog's reaction is likely to be different than when you are in or near the car. Of course, a dog may become aggressive in either situation. If the window of the car is left open, as it must be in hot weather, the dog may bite someone who gets close enough. If you're holding a small, shy, or fear-aggressive dog in your arms, you may get bitten if you try to calm him down when another dog or person approaches the car and he becomes agitated.

**Why does it happen?** If a dog is very protective of his owner and of himself, he will become increasingly more aggressive in a car. This is particularly true as he gets older. From his point of view the car belongs to him and it's another den in his territory. In his mind he is protecting his territory and his owner. These are the classic signs of territorial aggression. In some dogs the territorial aggression is combined with fear aggression, which adds to the intensity of his aggressive behavior.

It's a dog problem because of his aggressive temperament. It's a people problem because the dog has not been properly corrected or exposed to a variety of friendly people in the car. How many people will talk to you in your car with your dog barking and snarling at them? Not many will run the risk. As for corrections, it is very difficult to do in the car when you are in the front seat and the dog is in the back. What usually happens is the owner ends up yelling at the dog and finally giving him a whack. This, of course, never solves the problem.

Another aspect of the problem is the mixed messages given to the dog when he behaves aggressively in the car. In an effort to calm him down, the owner usually says, "It's okay, it's okay," as he or she pets him. So the dog keeps barking and growling and the owner keeps telling him it's okay. The dog does not understand his owner's words. He thinks he is being verbally praised for his response and consequently continues being aggressive.

It is also a people problem if the dog has never been obedience-trained and is not under control. He becomes even more territorial and more protective because he is *allowed* to act this way.

# 6

## Children and Aggressive Dogs

There is a special fantasy that many of us create when we are children or after we become parents. It is conjured up the first time we see a kid and a dog together. The image of little arms hugging little dogs slowly stirs into a gentle, emotional swirl. Given enough time and a lively imagination, the fantasy dog grows bigger as it trots alongside a boy or girl on a bike or splashes through the surf with a stick in its mouth. The fantasy ends with a nap of contentment at the end of the day, as the child curls up with a woolly friend and protector, the dream dog. The passage from daydream to reality is a seamless drift that is hardly noticed. Then one day, as if in a trance, we get a *real* dog. It all seems so right, because wherever we turn, popular culture tells us the dream is real. However, it only takes about twenty-four hours to discover that the dog of our dreams is not a stuffed toy, a cartoon character, or a canine actor. He is a living, breathing animal that eats, digests, runs, sleeps, barks, and reacts to people and his environ-

ment in loving and sometimes not-so-loving ways. The real problems begin when our illusions are dispelled by some of the unexpected realities of dog behavior. Eventually it becomes impossible to filter out the unpleasant facts that interfere with the fantasies. One undeniable truth is that more than a few dogs are dangerous around children, and if something isn't done about it, the consequences can be devastating. It is a fact that some dogs bite.

Sadly enough, the majority of dog-bite victims are children. Agencies and organizations that agree on this point include the American Medical Association (AMA), the Centers for Disease Control and Prevention in Atlanta (CDC), the American Veterinary Medical Association (AVMA), the Humane Society of the United States (HSUS), and the American Society for the Prevention of Cruelty to Animals (ASPCA). HSUS has joined with the U.S. Postal Service in sponsoring "National Dog Bite Prevention Week" each year from June 9 to 14. The CDC in Atlanta estimates that a total of 4.5 million dog bites occur each year in the United States, with more than 756,000 cases requiring medical attention. *Children make up over 60 percent of dog-bite victims.* This is probably because of their size, their energy level, their lack of knowledge about dog behavior, immature choices, and inadequate parental supervision around dogs.

Children are highly energetic, playfully curious, and at times oblivious to both the fear or pain they may cause a dog and the fact that the only defense the animal has is its teeth. Few children know about the dangers of hugging or approaching a dog from behind, touching his food bowl, pulling at his body, staring directly into his eyes, or trying to kiss him on the face. However, many children get bitten through no fault of their own. There are dogs that will bite the nearest person or child for reasons having to do with their aggressive temperaments.

Health-care providers believe that children suffer the most from dog bites and that 26 percent of dog bites in kids require medical attention, compared to 12 percent in adults. Three to 5 percent of dog bites are likely to cause secondary infections. In addition to injured tissue, dog bites can cause a wide range of bacterial and viral infections. The real horror, however, is that approximately twenty fatalities occur each year from dog attacks, and 60 percent of them are of children younger than ten years old.

## The Consequences of Having an Aggressive Dog

The consequences of having an aggressive dog in your home can be significant for the entire family but especially for the children. Parents must understand that when a dog attacks a child, he can cause serious injuries or, in some rare instances, fatality. At the very least, a dog bite is painful and frightening. If a dog growls, snarls, or curls his lip, his next action is to bite. When a dog sets in motion the signs of aggression, he is serious and will bite if you do not heed his warnings. Veterinarian Dr. Darlene White wrote in *Pet Health News*, "In addition to the physical and mental damage inflicted, dog bites can cause serious localized infections; tendon, joint and bone infections; and even fatal systemic infections. Crushing and tearing injuries often occur during an attack, and tissue death may result. Hospitalizations, wound debridement, intravenous antibiotics and physical therapy are often required following serious bite injuries. When you consider that a dog's jaw may exert between 200 to 450 pounds per square inch during a bite, it is not difficult to realize the potential danger present." Add to this the disfigurement that some dog-bite victims suffer and you have a grim set of circumstances for a child who has been attacked. Parents will not be able to live with themselves if their child is hurt because they disregarded the warning signs of aggression.

Lawsuits are another possibility if your dog bites your neighbor's child or a child visiting your home. A legal action of this nature can wipe you out financially if you do not have insurance for this situation. Another serious consequence is the possibility of a criminal charge based on abuse, for allowing a child to be harmed by a dog, knowing in advance the possible danger. The courts tend to be unsympathetic in such cases if they feel you had prior knowledge of your dog's aggressive nature. At the least, you may be served a court order to have your dog "put to sleep."

Parents who live with aggressive dogs must take their heads out of the sand and get out of the denial business. They must stop making excuses for their dogs' dangerous behavior. In the proper order of priorities a child's safety must come first. There can be no excuse for exposing children to the dangers of aggressive dogs. It is never acceptable to allow a family dog to display any form of aggressive behavior. The consequences are too frightening. Just as not all people are wonderful, not all dogs are wonderful. Parents must be realistic about this.

## Why Do These Problems Occur?

Canine aggression directed at children comes from dogs that are highly territorial and excessively protective of their domain. The same can be said of dogs that are not raised with children and are not used to them, or of dogs that have never been socialized. Some dogs are genetic misfits that are born with aggressive temperaments. There are aggressive dogs that have been made that way because they were themselves abused by being hit and yelled at on a continual basis. Dogs that have grown up with shy temperaments, that have been denied contact with people outside their immediate families, that have low pain tolerance, or that have been abused by children are walking time bombs that may go off at a child at any time.

Denial on the part of the dog owner and the failure to recognize the signs of aggression are the two biggest causes of aggressive-dog behavior toward children. Many dog owners have such a strong love for their dogs that their vision becomes clouded, and they are incapable of looking at their situation truthfully. Parents should ask themselves if they would allow their children to play with an aggressive dog if he wasn't part of their family. Would they permit their children to go near a dog that growled or snarled at them? The answer is obvious. Just because you love your dog doesn't mean he won't bite. Unfortunately, not all dogs like children. To avoid many of these problems you must acquire from a reliable source a well-bred dog that has been properly socialized, raised in a kind, happy environment, and brought up with children. You are more likely to have a wonderful relationship develop if you start out with a puppy and a child together. There is a great difference between a dog that has been raised with a child and one that has "been around children," as some people say when they are trying to get you to take a dog off their hands. Every dog is different. You must evaluate each and every dog individually to determine if he is child-safe. If you do not do this you may be making the greatest mistake of your life. See chapter 3, "How Aggressive *Is* Your Dog? Tests and Signs of Aggression."

## Some Aggressive-Behavior Problems Involving Children

**Problem:** Your dog acts aggressively toward your newborn child by growling, snarling, or with too much physical enthusiasm. Some dogs may innocently swipe the face of a child with their paws while exercising their curiosity or desire to play. A dog may be aggressive because he likes the child or because he feels threatened by the child's presence.

**Solutions:** If your dog is under six months, socialize him with the baby. This means taking him to the baby's room and introducing him to the baby's smells and possessions. Have the dog around the baby as much as possible, but only with your constant supervision. In these early situations keep a leash and collar on the dog and be ready to make a firm correction if necessary. When you are affectionate with your baby, show affection to the dog at the same time. Make sure the dog is obedience-trained and use the various commands to prevent him from jumping on the baby. "No!," "Sit," "Down," and "Stay" are the most helpful. Obedience-training is very important in order to maintain control whenever the two are together. If you are concerned about whether or not your dog will be aggressive around the baby, place him in a wire dog crate and observe his behavior. In any event, it is safest never to leave a baby or very young child alone in the same room with a dog. Place his leash and collar on him and make any necessary corrections along with a shake can correction if his behavior warrants it. See the Solutions Key in chapter 5, "Solving Your Dog's Aggressive-Behavior Problems."

If your dog is over six months, you may have to keep him away from the baby indefinitely by using the wire dog crate or keeping him in a dog run outside the house. You may be faced with the possibility of finding another home for your dog. Another possible solution is to buy a puppy (of the opposite sex only) as a second dog. A baby starting out life with a new puppy almost assures you of a quality situation with no aggression.

**Problem:** When your dog and your child play together, the dog play-bites. He doesn't understand that he causes pain.

**Solutions:** When a dog play-bites, he is essentially mouthing rather than biting. Mouthing is more annoying than dangerous, because the dog's teeth are merely brushing against the skin or clothing as his saliva makes a mess. This behavior can easily turn into a serious problem, however, and should not be permitted, because it can easily become intense and too aggressive. Your dog's play-biting problem is easy to solve while it is still a mild, playful activity. Simply administer a gentle leash correction or a verbal correction each time he does it. Your approach must be different if the play-biting becomes extreme, particularly if the dog is past six months of age and it is accompanied by other aggressive behaviors, such mounting, growling, or nipping. At that point you must administer severe or extra-firm leash corrections and verbal corrections. This requires that you assume a no-nonsense attitude. The intensity of your corrections must be equal to the severity of the dog's aggressiveness. See Leash Correction (1), Verbal Correction (3), and Muzzle (4) in the Solutions Key in chapter 5, "Solving Your Dog's Aggressive-Behavior Problems."

This behavior is usually the result of the child playing games that make the dog aggressive, such as tug-of-war. The problem can be avoided by instructing your child (and yourself) to use the following guidelines when playing with the dog: Do not roughhouse, do not slap him or hit him in any way, do not allow him to jump up on you, and do not incite aggressive behavior for the sake of having fun. Bear in mind that while the dog's reactions to your playful behavior are amusing, they can be dangerous for your child.

**Problem:** Your dog acts aggressively toward your children's friends when they try to play with him. He may growl, snap at them, block their path, or even push them with his body.

**Solutions:** Just because your dog tolerates *your* children does not mean he will tolerate other children in the house. If the visiting children are used to playing in a frisky manner with their own dogs, your less-than-tolerant dog may become aggressive. The age of the dog is an important factor. An aggressive dog less than six months of age is not usually dangerous because of his lack of maturity and full growth. However, when a young dog behaves aggressively, it is essential to apply a leash correction in addition to using the shake can. See Leash Correction (1) and Shake Can (7) in the Solutions Key in chapter 5, "Solving Your Dog's Aggressive-Behavior Problems."

**Children and Aggressive Dogs**

If the dog is past six months of age and you're not sure how aggressive he will be around visiting children, place him in a wire dog crate and watch his behavior when children are in the house. Look for the signs of aggression, some of which are intense barking, growling, or snarling. If the dog is aggressive toward children and you feel uncertain about him, keep him outdoors in a dog run, in a fenced-in area, or in some place separated from your visitors. Try giving him small amounts of food treats in order to create a positive association with visitors, especially children. See Leash Correction (1), Shake Can (7), Wire Dog Crate (5), and Use of Food (6) in the Solutions Key in chapter 5.

**Problem:** Your dog reacts aggressively when children tease him and pull on various parts of his body.

**Solutions:** The best approach is to use a reconditioning technique to increase the dog's tolerance for physical discomfort. This is accomplished by gently touching sensitive areas of his body, such as his loose skin, face, torso, legs, paws, rump, and tail. Try pulling gently on those areas, and if he does not react aggressively, praise him lavishly and, in some difficult cases, give him a food treat. As he accepts your pulling at him, keep raising the level of discomfort with gradual increases of intensity. Praise him or reward him with food each time he accepts the discomfort without growling, snarling, or snapping. Once you recondition your dog, he will not bite a child because he or she is playing a little rough or tugging at him. Remember the praise or the food reward is a very important part of this process. If the dog reacts aggressively to any of the pulls during the reconditioning process, give him a leash correction and a firmly stated "No!" If the dog is more than six months of age, use a soft muzzle if necessary.

Important preventive measures are teaching children the proper way to play with a dog and pet a dog. This means they must not approach the dog from behind, wrestle with him, chase him into corners or under tables, or pull at his body. The most important thing they must learn is to never tease the dog. Rather, they should pet the dog gently and lovingly. Under no circumstances should children be left alone with an aggressive dog. It is also well worth the effort to have a veterinarian examine the dog for hip dysplasia, arthritis, or any other medical problems. A dog will automatically snap if you touch a part of his body that is in pain.

**Problem:** The dog acts aggressively only with boys and is well behaved with girls.

**Solutions:** According to statistics, boys get bitten twice as often as girls. This is probably because they tend to be much rougher when playing with a dog than girls are. Boys are more likely to jump and pull on dogs and are prone to roughhousing with them. Playing rough with an aggressive dog is inviting a biting incident. If the boy is at least ten, get him involved with obedience-training his dog. If a boy learns how to work with a dog in training, it will give him some control of the dog, which helps prevent aggressive behavior. Teach him the proper way to play with a dog and keep on eye on him when they are together. Correct him when he mishandles the dog or plays too rough. Do not allow him to do anything nega-

**Children and Aggressive Dogs**

tive to the dog, such as hitting, kicking, punching, grabbing the tail, or jumping on him. Parents should also watch for displacement behavior. It is common for some kids (and some adults, also) to take out their anger and pent-up frustration on their dogs and treat them abusively even though it has nothing to do with the dog's behavior. And, finally, some children simply copy their parent's behavior.

**Problem:** While on the bed or the furniture, the dog growls, snaps, or bites when a child approaches or even enters the room.

**Solutions:** This problem also occurs with adults but is more frequently seen with children. Dogs tend to see children as littermates and aggressively assert themselves in order to establish a dominant position. Once you allow a dog on your bed or on a piece of furniture, he is going to claim it as his territory and become very protective of it. He will regard the bed or even the entire room as his and growl and snap when you approach. This is especially the case if the dog is territorial-aggressive or possessive-aggressive.

The obvious solution is prevention by not allowing the dog on the bed or the furniture in the first place. That means breaking him of the habit right away. You must establish a firm rule prohibiting him from being on the bed or on any furniture. This will require consistency on everyone's part. Use positive reinforcement techniques to get him off the bed and to come to you. Praise him lavishly and excitedly as you enter the room or use a motivator such as a toy to get him moving off the forbidden zones. It must be made clear that this is your territory, not his. If this does not solve the problem, then place a leash and collar on the dog and give him firm leash corrections whenever he behaves aggressively, whether it's on the bed or the sofa. Praise him after each correction and then walk him off furniture and out of the room. The obedience command "Place" is very useful in this situation. See chapter 4, "How to Obedience-Train an Aggressive Dog."

Unfortunately, you will not be able to correct the dog unless you actually catch him on the bed or sofa. Some dogs figure this out and hop off the minute they hear you coming. You can add to the solutions to this problem by creating an aversion to the furniture or bed. In other words, remove the attraction. Spread aluminum foil all over the surface of the furniture or the bed. The sound of it under his paws is surprising and the surface is slippery and unpleasant. A variation of this is the use of chicken wire spread across his favorite lounging area.

Get the dog a wire dog crate and make it as appealing as possible with a soft blanket or pillow. You can use it as an indoor doghouse with the door to the crate always open. You can also get him a dog basket or bed of his own and position it in a corner of a room of your choosing.

**Problem:** The dog is too dominant with your children. There's no respect between them. Even if they have grown up together, the dog does not show tolerance in many situations involving the children. He may push them with his body, butt them with his head, nip at their fingers, growl, or act menacing when he wants them to move away.

**Solutions:** It is essential for everyone in the family above the age of ten years to become dominant in the way they relate to the dog. Obviously, very young children are not going to be able to do this. However, once the children are ten, eleven, twelve years old, they can develop this ability by participating in the obedience-training of the dog. Once the dog is trained and everyone, including the children, can execute the commands, the dog will become more respectful. The dog must take a subordinate role in the family, but especially with the children if you are going to avoid canine aggression. The solution here lies in obedience-training with an emphasis on leash corrections and strong verbal corrections. If the dog is very aggressive or becomes aggressive when you try to train him, use a soft muzzle. A dog that is too dominant may try to bite a child that is attempting to correct him, and the muzzle becomes an important safety factor.

See Leash Correction (2), Verbal Correction (3), and Muzzle (4) in the Solutions Key in chapter 5, "Solving Your Dog's Aggressive-Behavior Problems."

**Problem:** The dog steals a toy and bites your child when he or she tries to take it back.

**Solutions:** It is necessary to keep the dog's toys separate from all children's toys. It is important to instruct children not to take their toys from the dog even if he stole them or took them when they weren't looking. Explain that this could make the dog bite, especially if they try to remove a toy from the dog's mouth. Explain to the child how the dog's mind works when he is territorial or possessive. See "Territorial/Overprotective Aggression" and "Possessive Aggression" in chapter 1, "Is Your Dog Aggressive?" Ask the child how he or she would feel if someone took from them toys they thought belonged to them. If the dog takes a toy that is not his, teach your child to have a parent retrieve it.

**Problem:** As the dog matures from puppyhood to adulthood he becomes more intolerant and aggressive with your child.

**Solutions:** Become familiar with the signs of aggression and understand that such behavior intensifies with age, making the dog more aggressive and consequently more dangerous. See "The Signs of Aggression" in chapter 3, "How Aggressive *Is* Your Dog? Tests and Signs of Aggression." Do not accept this behavior, believing that the dog will improve and become less aggressive with time. If you put your mind in a state of denial about your dog's aggressive behavior, you are only increasing the possibility of your child getting bitten. Your dog must be corrected immediately for any aggressive behavior, such as barking, growling, and even the slightest nipping. The most effective correction is the leash correction along with a verbal correction. If in your judgment the dog may bite your child, use a soft muzzle until you can change his aggressive behavior with dog obedience training as offered in chapter 4, "How to Obedience-Train an Aggressive Dog." In this instance neutering a male or spaying a female dog is an absolute essential.

See Leash Correction (2), Verbal Correction (3), and Muzzle (4) in the Solutions Key in chapter 5, "Solving Your Dog's Aggressive-Behavior Problems."

**Children and Aggressive Dogs**

**Problem:** The dog exhibits possessive-aggressive behavior when a child approaches you as you hold or pet him.

**Solutions:** Never allow a possessive-aggressive dog to stand next to you when your child approaches, especially if your dog is over one year of age and has shown signs of aggressive behavior. It is very important to condition your dog, if he is young, not to be allowed to show the signs of territorial or protective aggression. Dogs regard children as littermates and become possessive and protective of their territory or possessions if they are invaded or threatened in any way. Such dogs regard you as their possession and will become aggressive, even toward a child, if anyone gets too close. It is this behavior that is mistakenly identified as jealousy. Do not pet or praise your dog when he shows any sign of aggressive behavior, especially if your child is coming toward you. This gives the dog a mixed message. Your positive gestures and expressions only get him to believe it is okay to growl. You may be patting the dog and telling him, "Okay, okay," in order to tell him it's only your child and he shouldn't get upset. The effect, however, is to reward him for his aggressive behavior. The best way to deal with this is to have a food or toy motivator ready with which to entice him. When your child approaches, reward your dog with a food treat or a toy he enjoys. Eventually your dog will think of your child's approach (with or without you) as a positive experience. Your dog will associate getting a treat or some playtime with your child and in that way will not be defensive or territorial.

**Problem:** Your dog is not familiar with small children. Unexpectedly he finds himself in the company of a visiting baby or child and becomes aggressive. He may give a menacing growl from deep in his throat in his first encounter. He may also lunge at the visitor and bark excessively, baring his teeth.

**Solutions:** Keep your dog away from all children until you can determine how he will behave with them. When in the presence of children it is essential to have your dog on a leash and training collar so that you can give him a leash correction for any sign of aggression whatsoever. Use a soft muzzle if the dog's aggressive potential is severe, in order to prevent any possible injuries. Place the dog in a wire dog crate when children come to visit or place him behind a puppy gate if it is strong enough to confine him. If the dog is very aggressive, place him outdoors in a dog run so that you can see how he reacts to children without fear of them getting hurt. Unless your dog has been raised with children, you must not assume he will behave properly when they come to see you. Being "around children" is not the same as living with them and offers no guarantee that the dog is safe in that situation. Even a dog raised with children may not accept visiting children and may become aggressive toward them.

See Leash Correction (2), Verbal Correction (3), and Muzzle (4) in the Solutions Key in chapter 5, "Solving Your Dog's Aggressive-Behavior Problems."

**Children and Aggressive Dogs**

## A Child's Guide to Bite Prevention

### Body Language That Warns You

A dog's body language usually, but not always, indicates that he is seriously considering an attack. The following stances displayed by a dog are offered by him as a warning to whomever he has focused his attention on, and it should be heeded.

1. A dominant-aggressive dog's pose consists of erect ears, a stiff body, a tail held high, and fur that is raised up from the body, referred to as having his "hackles up."
2. A fearful-aggressive dog's pose consists of ears that are flattened back, a crouched body, the head held low, and the tail tucked between the legs.
3. Body language seen in both dominant-aggressive and fearful-aggressive dogs are growls and mean-sounding barks, snarls or lifted lips, and bared teeth.

**The Shy or Fearful Dog.** A dog that is shy or fearful takes a defensive posture that means he is trying to protect himself and will become aggressive. This behavior is easy to recognize because he is easily frightened by new people, places, or experiences. Anything unfamiliar will set him off into a barking or growling tantrum with his ears back and his tail either between his legs or wagging with excitement. He will appear to face you down until you move toward him, and then he may seem to retreat only to go for you the minute you stop or turn away. His goal is to frighten you away, but if you do not go, he will attack. Despite his apparent fear of you, he is dangerous, and you must not go near him. He will bite out of fear if you approach him or even relate to him in any way. Leave him alone and walk away slowly.

**The Dominant Dog.** A dog that is truly aggressive is very dominant, assertive, threatening, and overconfident, and his aggression is on a hair trigger. His posture is designed to make him look even bigger than he is by displaying a puffed-up look with raised fur and parts of his body held erect. He may stand sideways rather than straight on in order to show you his full size. He will stare in the most menacing way and at first make a low-sounding growl from deep within his throat. At that point he may start moving slowly toward you if you move. He may also snarl and bare his teeth. A dominant dog in this state is dangerous and ready to attack you. Although it is essential to get away from him, you must not run. It is safer to slowly back away without turning around until there is a great distance between you. Although you must not turn away from the dog as you back off, it is imperative not to make eye contact with him, as this constitutes a challenge that will have the opposite effect that you want.

## Avoiding Dog Bites

Most dog bites can be prevented by understanding what you should and should not do. The following thirteen suggestions will help a great deal.

1. If a strange dog enters your front lawn or backyard, do not approach him, do not shoo

**Children and Aggressive Dogs**

him away, and do not talk to him. Go indoors
and get help from an adult.

2.  Never approach a strange dog that is alone,
    confined to his own yard, or tied up.

3.  Do not pet someone else's dog without
    permission from the owner and permission
    from the dog. If the owner tells you it's okay,
    then approach the dog from a side angle rather
    than from directly in front of him and never
    from behind. Do not approach with quick, jerky
    motions. Speak in a normal tone of voice and
    do not try to play with him. You do not want
    the dog to get excited or worried or frightened
    of you. Fold your fingers together as though
    you were making a fist and gently offer it to
    the dog with your knuckles first. This protects
    your fingers from being bitten and is

nonthreatening to the dog. The dog's body language will tell you if he gives you permission to say hello or not. If he is interested, the dog will extend himself to you and sniff your knuckles. You may now talk to the dog and pet him without bringing your hand down over the top of his head. You have just made a new friend. Another possibility is that the dog may turn away from your hand and try to avoid you. This is a very gentle warning to stop. The dog may be frightened or for some unknown reason unfriendly. Do not try to pet an unfriendly dog, one that does not give you permission.

4. Do not run past a strange dog, because it sets in motion his hunting instincts, and he will chase you. You can never be sure how he will behave once he catches up. If a dog chases you, it is best to stand still. The dog is probably going to lose interest once he takes a sniff and realizes you are not a threat.

5. Stay away from a dog when he is eating and do not go near his food or water bowls when he is not eating, even if you participate in the dog's feeding routine.

6. Avoid making eye-to-eye contact with a strange dog or one that is staring at you, growling at you, or threatening you in any way. Dogs that stare at each other are challenging each other.

7. Do not disturb a sleeping dog, especially if he is known to be aggressive.

**Children and Aggressive Dogs**

8. Stay away from a mother dog when she is looking after her puppies, especially if they are drinking milk from her breasts.

9. Always keep your dog on a leash when you are outdoors walking him.

10. If your dog gets into a fight with another dog, do not try to separate them on your own. If your dog is on-leash, pull him away but do not lift him up or the other dog will attack you in an effort to get at him. It takes a water hose or a broom to break up a dogfight, and it must be done by an adult.

11. Do not play games with any dog that involve his mouth. This includes tug-of-war, using sticks, old socks, dog toys of every sort, old shoes, and especially bones and food items.

12. Never tease any dog, especially one that is confined or tied down in some way.

13. If you come upon an injured dog, do not touch him. Get help from an adult. Dogs in pain may snap at anyone who touches them where it hurts.

## What to Do If a Dog Attacks

Summon up all the courage you have, take a deep breath, and try to stand as stiff as a board if the dog is just threatening you. Do not run. Do not stare him in the eyes. Try not to panic and try to think like the person in charge. In the deepest voice you can manage tell the dog to go home or to sit, but do not make any gestures with your hands or your arms. Keep them at your side with your fingers close together. Stand perfectly still until the dog loses interest. When he does, do not turn your back on him. Slowly back away until you are at a safe distance from him.

If the dog does attack you, give him something to bite on like your coat or your schoolbag or whatever you may be holding. If you are on a bike, keep it between you and the dog. The idea is to place whatever obstacle you can between you and the dog. If he takes the bait and becomes involved with the decoy that you gave him to chew on, then slowly back away until you are safe. Get help from an adult.

If the dog jumps on you and knocks you to the ground, curl up into a ball like a baby that is still inside its mother's stomach. Lie facedown and cover your ears with your hands. Keep your fingers tightly closed. Screaming or moving around continues his interest in you, so try not to do that. Once the dog determines that you are no longer a threat to him he will lose interest and back off. Do not move until you are sure he is gone or until help arrives. Report the incident to your parents, who should file a report to the police, the local health department, and the agency responsible for animal control.

Although the information, advice, and instruction offered here and throughout this guide are given without apologies, it is not the purpose of this book to discourage anyone from living with a dog. It is our greatest wish to help dogs and people learn how to live together with the quiet enjoyment of a life without fear or danger. When you know what to do to change or manage the unpleasant and disturbing aspects of some dogs and some people, you are better able to enjoy your lives together as you always wanted. There is a great pleasure and satisfaction to be had when dogs and humans accord each other love, respect, and harmony.

# 7

## Decisions — What to Do If Your Dog Growls or Bites

If your dog growls or bites, the first step toward solving the problem is accepting the fact that he is aggressive and that something must be done about it. Aggressive behavior in dogs is a serious problem that must be addressed by those responsible for him. Do not make excuses for his behavior and do not go into a state of denial, with statements such as "He is a wonderful dog except that he has this little growling problem" or "He only bites occasionally, but it's not serious because he never breaks the skin." Once you accept the fact that your dog's behavior is a problem, you are on the way to solving it and are halfway home. With this in mind, here are the things that you should do:

1. Find out if your dog's aggressive behavior is caused by a medical problem. See a veterinarian and have your dog examined thoroughly. Does

he have bad hips, does he have a thyroid condition, or does he have a low tolerance for pain and discomfort? Many dogs will snap or bite if you touch them in a place that hurts.

2.  Contact the dog's breeder and ask if there is any history of aggressive behavior in the line, particularly in the dog's parents or grand-parents. Ask if any other dogs from his litter displayed aggressive behavior. This would suggest that your dog's aggressive behavior is inherited and that you must gain control of him through obedience training and accept the fact that his behavior cannot be permanently changed.

3.  If the dog was purchased from a private source or from a rescue shelter, try to get as much behavior history as possible, with a strong focus on aggressive behavior. The point is to determine if his aggressive behavior is inherited or not.

4.  Contact a professional dog trainer or animal behaviorist, one who is qualified to work with aggressive behavior in dogs and has experience in this very specialized field. Engage the services of one that uses only positive training techniques as described in chapter 4, "How to Obedience-Train an Aggressive Dog." It is wise to get at least three separate evaluations from three different trainers.

5.  Make a commitment to obedience-train your dog no matter what the cause of his aggressive behavior, and then decide how to do it.

## Four Ways to Train Your Dog

1. *Do it yourself.* With the help of books, tapes, or seminars, it is not difficult to train your own aggressive dog. Chapters 4 and 5 of this book offer the best instruction and guidance available for this purpose.

2. *Training classes.* In this situation, an instructor teaches and guides you along with a group of dogs and their owners. The most important benefit of a training class, apart from the training, is that your dog will have an opportunity to become more socialized because of the exposure to other people and their dogs. Some classes, however, will not accept your dog if his level of aggression represents a danger to others in the class. This usually applies to aggressive dogs one year or older.

3. *Private training in your home.* In this situation a professional trainer comes to your home to train your dog and work with you in the environment where the aggressive behavior occurs. Working on specific aggressive-behavior problems, such as food aggression or territorial aggression, with the entire family in the home is effective and beneficial. When you hire a professional in-home dog trainer, it is important that he train your aggressive dog, rather than training you to train the dog. In-home training for aggressive dogs costs between $500 and $1,500, depending on the severity of the problem.

4. *In-kennel training (boarding and training).* This is a highly successful method for aggressive dogs that growl or bite, that are one year or older, and that are potentially dangerous. Obedience training in a sleep-away kennel provides the dynamic of everyday handling from an experienced and varied group of trainers and handlers in addition to exposure to many different dogs. In-kennel training is effective because it allows the trainers to work with a dog away from his owners, who often contribute to the problem inadvertently through lack of experience or excessive emotions. In-kennel trainers are more easily able to identify the type of aggressive behavior of a dog and its cause and then work with him on a daily basis with training techniques that are customized for his problems. In-kennel training provides obedience training, behavior modification, and much needed socialization with people and dogs. The cost of this service ranges from $1,500 to $5,000, depending on the dog's size, age, and health needs, and the severity of his problem.

## Selecting a Trainer

The most important decisions to be made are training your dog, deciding how to do it, and selecting the right trainer. If you are not going to train your dog yourself, interview the prospective trainer and ask for referrals from satisfied clients, veterinarians, breeders, and professional dog groomers. Here is a list of questions we suggest you ask your prospective trainer:

1. How many years have you been in business?
2. How many dogs have you trained professionally?
3. Where did you get your training? Have you graduated from a certified dog-training school?
4. What methods do you use? Are they positive and nonabusive in nature?
5. Do you use fear to train a dog? Do you hit the dog, use electric shock devices, or any other methods that involve pain?
6. Are you a hands-on trainer? Do you work with the dog yourself and not just tell me, the client, what to do?
7. Can you provide three referrals for aggressive dogs that you have trained?
8. How long is the training course and what is the price?
9. What do you teach besides focusing on the aggressive problem? Do you include obedience training (a must for all dogs, aggressive or not).
10. What type of guarantee, if any, do you offer?
11. Are follow-up visits or consultations included in the price?
12. What type of liability insurance do you carry in case you get bitten?

## Investing in Your Dog

Many people do not train their dogs, even when they are aggressive. Some believe the dog will somehow improve with age and become mellow with the passage of time. This notion is incorrect and dangerous. Statistics show that most bites are from dogs one year of age and older. If you live with an aggressive dog, you must consider the consequences if your dog bites you, a member of your family, a child, or any other person. First and foremost is the pain and suffering of the victim and how that affects you emotionally. The guilt can linger for the rest of your life because of what your dog did to another person. Then there is the liability you face, which can become ruinous if you are not insured. In some communities you can be prosecuted for criminal negligence. You certainly can be sued in civil court for immediate and long-term medical expenses, pain and suffering, loss of property, loss of employment, permanent disabilities, and much more. As you can imagine, these claims can add up quickly into the high end of six figures.

If your dog is aggressive, it is a major investment to have him trained. Some people have trouble justifying the expense of dog training, but that is amazing considering how much most dog owners are willing to spend when their dog becomes sick. Many dog owners will spend almost any amount of money to keep their pets healthy. The point is that if the dog has emotional problems, why won't you spend the same amount to save his life and ensure the safety of those who come in contact with him? A dog that continually bites people will eventually be euthanized either by court order or as the only choice available to you as the dog's owner. If you consider the cost of owning a dog over a ten-year period, including the initial purchase price, food, medical care, grooming, boarding, and toys, $7,000 to $8,000 would be a conservative estimate. A more extravagant estimate would be around $20,000. The cost of obedience training is as much a necessity as any of the previously mentioned items. Perhaps you owe it to your best friend to do all that is possible to control his behavior, which will not only prevent people from getting hurt but possibly save his life. You should ask yourself if you love your dog enough to make an investment that will ensure his behaving properly so that he can spend the rest of his natural life with his family.

## Negative Consequences of Having an Aggressive Dog

When you have an extremely aggressive dog, there are difficult situations with which you must deal. At such times you may have to ask yourself if obedience training can cure the problem. Most likely you will only be able to control your dog's behavior, rather than permanently change it. The important question is whether or not you can trust your dog completely. Aggressive dogs bite more children than adults, and if you live in a home with children, you must consider whether or not they are safe around your dog. Are your children's friends safe around your dog? These are important questions even after the dog has been trained. This is a heart-wrenching subject to deal with for anyone in this position.

Look at the situation objectively. Would you allow your child or family to visit a home where the dog is likely to bite? The answer is obvious if the dog involved is not your own. Sometimes the only choice you have is to find a home without children for your biting dog. An aggressive dog you cannot trust completely around children may need a more isolated environment, which offers fewer opportunities to bite anyone. This is a family matter that requires input from everyone involved. We suggest you call on professional people such as dog trainers or veterinarians to help guide you through this process. There are sixty million dogs in the United States, and some of them are genetically defective animals who grow up to be unreliable and dangerous. This is a fact that is very difficult to apply to an individual dog that may happen to be yours. The fact is, there are stories reported in the media on a regular basis about such dogs that have seriously attacked people and in some cases have even caused death.

There is a need to be honest with yourself if your dog is aggressive and potentially dangerous to your family, your friends, your neighbors, or innocent strangers. Are you frightened of your own dog, and if so, is there any hope for him? The sad truth is that sometimes there isn't. It is extremely difficult to consider "putting your dog to sleep." This is a decision that must be thought out carefully and requires that you go to all the sources available to help you. Consult a dog trainer, animal behaviorist, your own veterinarian, or the breeder who brought the animal into the world.

Life is precious, and this is one of the most difficult decisions anyone can make. Emotions can be intense, so you must examine every possibility and make sure that all avenues have been explored before reaching a conclusion and coming to the right decision. We sincerely hope that this is not your situation. If it is, then it is your responsibility to do the right thing.

The behavior of most aggressive dogs can be either modified or managed in such a way as to minimize their problems. There is no reason why you shouldn't be able to change your aggressive dog's behavior and thus change the quality of your life, provided you have accepted and put into action all that is offered in this guide.

If you have reached this paragraph, it can only mean you have read all that is here and, we assume, have done the work with your dog that is necessary to turn things around. For that we congratulate you and offer our sincere admiration. Only dog owners who truly love their dog and feel a sense of responsibility to their community will recognize that their dog has a problem and then choose to do something about it. Consider the training and the solutions we offer you as the first step toward change for the better. Take a deep breath and give yourself a well-deserved pat on the back. From here on, your job is to practice what you've learned and stay bonded with your dog. Keep a watchful eye and go back to the appropriate material in this book if and when your dog shows any other sign of aggression. You will succeed.

GRRR!